GW00357819

THESE TRUTHS CAN CHANGE YOUR LIFE

BY

Joseph Murphy, D.D., Ph.D., LL.D., D.R.S.

DeVorss & Co., *Publishers*
P.O. Box 550
Marina del Rey, California 90294-0550

ISBN: 0-87516-476-5
Library of Congress Card Catalog Number: 81-71208

Second Printing, 1986

Printed in the United States of America

CONTENTS

CHAPTER 1

A Visit to China, Hong Kong and Tokyo

In the latter part of 1980 I joined a group of tourists who were going on the same journey to see the various cities of China, called the People's Republic of China. It is true that China has been experiencing a transformation which has taken root everywhere—in the farms called communes, hotels, restaurants, schools, hospitals and colleges. The people are very friendly, and the guides we had spoke excellent English. We watched a teacher conducting a class on English, and she was very competent. She explained that all students in the higher grades learn English as a secondary language. A visit to the main hospital in Peking proved most interesting and instructive. The chief physician (who spoke six languages fluently) explained their success with acupuncture.

The treatment of visitors is invariably friendly, thoughtful and courteous. The various guides we had on this trip explained that their written language—using a unique, nonalphabetic script—links all parts of modern China. The written language remains constant throughout the land. In the spoken form, however, Chinese has numerous dialects. This is why the guide in Peking said to me, "I can't go with you to Canton, as I don't understand their dialect." He also said that about two-thirds of the people speak Mandarin—the national dialect. They have about five major dialects in the country, however. Salaries average about sixty yuan a month, which is equivalent to about forty-five dollars. Remember, the cost of living is commensurately low.

A visit to one of their large communes proved to be very interesting and illuminating. The foreman of the commune addressed us, stating that about fifty thousand people operated that particular collective farm. There was an incentive for each worker: If he produced more and was diligent and industrious in his work, he would receive more money based on what they call units of labor. Country families are encouraged to grow their own vegetables and to care for some animals, such as sheep and goats, both for their own consumption and for sale at the rural market. The great percentage of agricultural production is carried out in collectively owned fields, and income is distributed according to individual output. A certain sum of money is set aside for medical care, pensions, social services and education. The state owns everything.

VISIT TO CHINA, HONG KONG AND TOKYO

How He Won His Freedom

While talking with an old friend of mine in Hong Kong, a gentleman with whom I have had business dealings and with whom I have corresponded for about ten years, I learned for the first time that he had been born in China, had studied in a missionary school when young, and had a burning desire to go to Hong Kong. But all of his friends who had tried to escape to that city were either drowned in the attempt to swim the treacherous waters or were shot by guards who knew they were trying to escape the regime. He said that he prayed to Buddha to show him the way. He also asked the I Ching,* which he inherited from his grandfather. The hexagram he received said, "It furthers you to cross the water—good fortune." This was an auspicious prognostication, and so, he, with another friend, found a boat and succeeded in landing at a remote part of the island. Today he is very successful and now employs a great number of people. He said, "I beat the established laws and rules." He proved the power of faith in the Invisible Presence and Power Which is omnipotent and omniscient.

**The I Ching or Book of Changes,* Wilhelm/Baynes Edition, Princeton University Press, Princeton, N.J., 1967. See also *Secrets of the I Ching* by Joseph Murphy, Parker Publishing Company, West Nyack, N.Y., 1970.

Special Privileges

During a conversation with an Englishman who has lived for many years in China and who is now handling and directing a British corporation in Southern China, I was told that the common people, called peasants, get very upset and angry about the special privileges of high-ranking officials. He said that the old saying in China is still prevalent: "Once a man is promoted, even his dogs and his chickens go to heaven." This practice still permeates society. We saw in every city we visited men and women in private limousines with private chauffeurs and blinds drawn in the car. On inquiry, we were invariably told that he or she was a member of the communist hierarchy. It seems that all members of the communist party get special privileges that they have no desire to relinquish.

Failure of Egalitarianism

Those who assert or promote the view that men are equal politically, socially, spiritually, or in any other way are absurd and ludicrous. One of the men who spoke to us at one of the communes explained that the men who produced more and accomplished more are promoted as a result and receive more pay. They arrange incentives for the workers on the basis that the chance to get richer will make people work harder.

The commune leader realizes that all men are not equal. And it is true that all people are not equal.

Some men are tall and strong, others are weak and short. Some have the gift of music, others have not. Some are born with great psychic endowment, others are not. Some boys today have a far higher IQ than others. Emerson tells us that the chemist can tell his secrets to the carpenter because the carpenter is not equal to him in the science of chemistry. Likewise, the chemist is not equal to the carpenter in his knowledge of construction, mensuration and other techniques.

Look around you and you find children born into a lovely home where peace and love reign supreme and where parents practice the Presence of God regularly. Children grow up in the image and likeness of the dominant mental, emotional and spiritual climate of the home. Such children have a great advantage over children born into a home where they are unwanted, unloved, and where turmoil and dissension exist between the parents.

Inequality is rampant throughout all nature. The mouse is not equal to the horse, the lamb is not equal to the lion, etc. The hill is not equal to the high mountains and the small lake is not equal to the sea. Theoretically, we are all equal before the law in the U.S.A., but, as you know very well, if there is an unjust judge administering the law, it doesn't always turn out that way.

It is true that we are equal in the eyes of God and that riches are of our mind. If we use our mind wisely and constructively, according to spiritual values and principles which are eternal, we then prove that riches, justice, health and happiness result from that usage. If we think good, good will follow. In nature the flowers are not equal; neither are the trees, rivers, stars, suns and moons.

The Truth Is Always the Same

Truth never changes. It is the same yesterday, today and forever. A Chinese guide with whom I got very friendly knew and understood the Communist Manifesto very well. It states that war between the communists and the bourgeois society of which we are a part is inevitable and will continue until the whole world becomes communistic. A student of the laws of mind knows that if war is your premise and the dominant factor in your mind, you will create war, as the Russians have done in Afghanistan and in other places. This is of their own choice, their purpose and plan.

This young man admitted that he was a former Red Guard. He denounced professors, linguists, teachers, scientists and the elite of China. He abused them, gave them menial jobs in farms and factories, and looted and burned some old temples and churches. He now realizes that the Red Guard caused untold damage to the cultural, scientific and industrial progress of China. He has now changed and wants to study physics in America or London so that he can contribute to the expansion and growth of his country. He said to me, "When we are young and brainwashed, we possess heads but no brains."

Classless Society

This idea is an absolute farce and an insult to the intelligence of a seven-year-old boy who is coming into the age of reason. Stalin of the U.S.S.R. and Mao of China (incidentally, they are taking down his pictures and statues all over China) tried to abolish classes in society by liquidating all those who opposed their collectivist dream. The theory behind this is that the proletarian class (which originally meant the poorest and lowest class in a community or state; one with no property and belonging to the wage-earning class) will be in charge and dominant; and, gradually, over a period of time, there will develop a classless society.

This, of course, is called the big lie, palpably false and too stupid for words. It might be looked upon as one of the great illusions of brainwashed people who do not know the laws of mind and the way of Infinite Spirit. The only condition in which there are no opposites is in the Absolute, and this can never be experienced in human existence.

An inevitable duality besets all nature. We have ebb and flow, in and out, sweet and bitter, hard and soft, male and female, positive and negative, night and day, darkness and light, motion and rest, yea and nay, and fear and love. Life is one, but it functions as a duality. Emerson explained it so lucidly when he said, "Polarity, or action and reaction, we meet in every part of nature." Infinite differentiation is the law of life. There can never be a classless society.

I once taught a class in chemistry. Some of the boys in the class were very eager to learn; they studied, applied themselves, were idealistic and wanted to accomplish great things in the world. Others were lazy, however. They refused to study, spent time in the pool hall and were generally indifferent. There was nothing wrong with their IQ, but there was something wrong with their choices. . . . *Choose you this day whom ye will serve* . . . (Joshua 24:15).

All evil ultimately destroys itself. "The mills of the gods grind slowly but they grind exceedingly fine." Tyrants, dictators and despots who engage in suppression of the masses, ruthlessly liquidating millions of people, will, of course, experience a reaction of the law themselves. The Bible says: *I will overturn, overturn, overturn, it: and it shall be no more, until he come whose right it is; and I will give it him* (Ezekiel 21:27).

What should govern and reign supreme in our mind are the spiritual values of life which are eternal. All of us are here to grow, expand, move forward in the light, and express more and more of our Divinity. When we misuse the law, we get into trouble and difficulties of all kinds. Change eternal is at the root of all things, and it is through change that we evolve. Truth may be submerged for a while, but it inevitably will rise triumphant.

You are here to reconcile the opposites. If you are sick, you can call on the healing power of God to make you well. If you have sufficient faith in God, a healing will follow quickly; if not, go to a doctor at once and bless him. If you are poor, you can claim that God's riches are circulating in your life, and, when wealthy, you have reconciled the opposites. You can cast out fear by filling your mind with the truths of the 91st Psalm and you are no longer fearful.

Communistic teaching has forgotten the power of God in man, and this is the great flaw and perversion which permeates their entire teaching and propaganda.

You Are Living in a Spiritual World

God indwells you. God is omnipresent and must, therefore, be the Reality of you. A monk in China said to me through an interpreter that the people in the country worship and pray and will always continue to do so. I asked one guide: "Do the people practice Buddhism?" He laughed and said, "Our religion is Marxism and Leninism, but the rank and file don't accept it." I knew what he meant, but he gave the standard answer to such questions.

According to the communistic regime, economic

determination is paramount. They hold and teach that your mental attitude and general thinking are caused by externals, such as environment and conditions. In other words, your consciousness (the way you think, feel, believe and whatever you give mental consent to) is molded and fashioned by circumstances and conditions.

All of this is a half-truth in the sense that millions of people are governed by environmental belief, early training, conditions and circumstances. This is called the law of averages. But there are millions of people all over the world who, although born in its slums and ghettos, have become famous in the fields of science, art, literature and medicine and have also become great leaders and statesmen. They refused to think according to the law of averages. They tuned in on the Infinite and brought forth great inventions and discoveries along all lines.

I knew a great surgeon in New York who had been born in the slums. His mother was a prostitute and he didn't know his father. He listened to what the clergyman said at a local school and refused to be bound by environmental suggestion. He imagined himself to be a great doctor and surgeon and worked to bring this to pass. He said to me, "I asked God to guide me, direct me and show me the way. Millions like this surgeon have also learned the other half of the great truth: that your thought and feeling control your destiny. Your subconscious reproduces your habitual thinking and imagery, creating circumstances and experiences. In other words, you are what you think all day long.

Voice Crying in the Wilderness

There is an inner voice that speaks to all men throughout the world. It is the inner urge of the Divine Presence in man urging him to release his talents to the world and express more and more of his God-like powers. It is that inner voice in you that says to rise, transcend and grow; come on up higher, I have need of you. God is seeking a holy receptacle through you so that by using you He might express Himself at higher levels.

My observation is that where the communist regime governs it makes millions of people serfs, slaves and clods. The means used to submerge the ideas and inner desires of people is that of force, as through the barrel of a gun, which will ultimately bring about absolute failure resulting in the liberation of all those people. The premise (force), being false, determines the result, which must be failure.

The truth student is against false ideas in the mind, not with people. All ideas not born of God must be false, for God is love. All of us must look within to the One, the Beautiful and the Good, dwelling on the eternal truths and the great spiritual values of life; then we shall grow in wisdom, truth and beauty and become strong in God. When we do this and make a habit of it, God will rise in all of us and the enemies of fear, hate, resentment, doubt and compromise will be dissolved in the light of God's love.

The Principle of Divine Right Action

In talking with a man from Texas on our tour of China, he told me that for many years he had possessed a marvelous idea, an invention which would be a great boon and blessing to the organization for which he works, but that its introduction was blocked at every turn. I asked him where his idea came from, and he replied that this invention came to him in his sleep and was obviously a very good invention.

The explanation is ofttimes the cure. He admitted that he was very resentful of the executive vice president in charge of operations, whom he blamed for blocking his idea. I explained to him that actually he was blocking his own good, because to hold an ideal in his mind and at the same time resent the vice president for blocking it is to make a god of the vice president, thereby worshipping false gods. I pointed out that the vice president had no power to block his good and that he was transferring the power to him. The only power is of God, Which is omnipotent; therefore, he was unjust to himself because he had a false god.

I gave him this prayer: "The ideal I have in my mind is a gift of God. It is good and very good. What God gives, He manifests and brings forth in

Divine law and order. I give all power to the God-Presence within. It is done. It is finished and I give thanks."

Yesterday I received a grateful letter from him saying that the company had accepted his novel idea. He removed his resentment from his mind and acknowledged no enemy to the power of the Infinite within him.

You Must Be Before You Can Have

You possess nothing but by right of consciousness. I explained the meaning of this to a young lady who wants to become a doctor. She was rejected by five different medical institutions so far, each claiming that it was full. She began to see that she must mentally act as though it were already accomplished and pictured herself studying in medical school. I suggested that she look at a diploma on the wall, stating that she is a physician and surgeon in the State of California and hear the writer congratulate her on her graduation as a physician.

In prayer you always go to the end and, having seen and felt the end, you have willed the means to the realization of the end. She thus played the role in her mind and acted as though it were an accomplished fact. Our interview was about five months ago, and the way suddenly opened up for her to attend in Montreal, Canada.

Whatsoever a Man Soweth,
That Shall He Also Reap

All of us are familiar with the great truth that whatever we impress or impregnate in our subconscious mind, whether good or bad, will come forth into objective manifestation. This is the law of mind. Look upon it as being as invariable and inflexible as are the laws of mathematics or chemistry. You must realize there is only One Law in all its various phases and functions.

While building a bridge, an engineer must conform to the principles of mathematics and the laws of stress and strain. The chemist must conform to the principles of chemistry and understand laws of attraction and repulsion. He must also understand the role of atoms and molecules. He doesn't try to change the principles of chemistry any more so than the electrical engineer tries to change the principles of electricity.

Plant, therefore, in your mind whatsoever things are lovely, noble, dignified and Godlike. . . . *Unto every one that hath shall be given* . . . (Matthew 25:29). This means that what you claim and feel to be true in your mind will be given to you. What a person has is not his material possessions but a state of mind, a mental attitude or deep-seated conviction. Remember, everything you possess in a material way, such as your home, stocks, bonds, land, etc., is a mathematical, accurate reflection of your mental state. In other words, what you psychologically possess will be made manifest on the screen of space.

There is no such thing as chance. All is law. There are no accidents. All is law and a mathematical, accurate reflection of your state of consciousness. Consciousness is the sum total of our conscious and subconscious assumptions, beliefs and convictions. In other words, it is the sum total of our conscious and subconscious acceptances.

It Is Wise to Tell No Man

It is foolish to talk about your dreams, aspirations, plans and secret desires with others. Your prayer is with the Father within. Whatever you claim and feel to be true in the silence of your soul, the Spirit in you will validate and honor and bring to pass. It is foolish to pluck a flower before it blooms and blossoms. This does not mean that when you go to a doctor, psychologist or attorney you do not tell him your problem, because he is there to help you and cooperate with you. What you convey to a clergyman or doctor is a secret, and he or she keeps that information in confidence.

A girl in a local office was telling everybody recently that she was going to marry the boss and that she had an engagement ring, yet it was another girl in the office who actually married the boss. Keep your own counsel and stop talking about something that has not yet happened. There is the man who is always talking about the home he is going to build, the book he is going to write, and the vast amount of money he is going to make. You can rest assured he never accomplishes any of these things he is bragging and boasting about. The man who writes a book sits down and writes it, has it published and then tells you about it. Withhold your speech until results speak for themselves.

A great number of people dissipate the force of excellent resolutions by talking too much about them. A young man in a local bank was promised a promotion to executive vice president. He told his wife about it, but forgot to tell her to keep it confidential until it had happened. She told all her friends as well as his friends in the bank, and the wives of the other men in the bank created such an uproar, claiming their husbands had seniority, etc., that he never did receive the promotion.

Make it a point to mind your own business. It is called "MYOB." You will find it very profitable. Be sure you do not tell your relatives or your so-called best friend your secret prayer. Your best friend is God. A college teacher told me that she told her immediate family that she was going around the world on a guided cruise costing seven thousand dollars. They immediately poured ice cold water on the idea. A brother wanted to borrow money for his family business and said she should lend him the money. Others claimed they needed money for an operation, etc. Instead of rejoicing in her good fortune and wishing her a *bon voyage,* they resented the trip and tried to prevent it. Nevertheless, she went on the cruise and is much wiser now. Go, and tell no man.

Predicting My Future

Thou madest him to have dominion over the works of thy hands . . . (Psalm 8:6). I know that my faith in God determines my future. My faith in God means my faith in all things good. I unite myself now with true ideas and I know the future will be in the image and likeness of my habitual thinking. "As a man thinketh in his heart, so is he." "Whatsoever things are true, whatsoever things are honest, whatsoever things are just, whatsoever things are lovely, and of good report," day and night I meditate on these things, and I know that these seeds (thoughts) which I habitually dwell upon will become a rich harvest for me. I am the captain of my own soul; I am the master of my fate; for my thought and feeling are my destiny.

CHAPTER 2

Do You Have Free Will?

We had a most interesting trip to Chengtu, a beautiful city, with its temperate climate, broad streets and many public parks. It is a center of handicrafts and was known as the City of Brocade under the Han Dynasty. Local buses in this city are run entirely on natural gas stored in bags on top at a cost of one cent for sixty miles. In one of the factories, where everything seems to be done by hand, I chatted with one of the workers who had formerly lived in New York City and who had at one time listened to a series of lectures by the late Dr. Emmet Fox. For obvious reasons, he does not promulgate his knowledge of the laws of mind. I also found that some of the monks in the many monasteries have an excellent knowledge of the scriptures of the world.

He Keeps His Vessel Covered

This worker I spoke of knows the meaning of Moses' injunction to the children of Israel to "never leave any vessel uncovered." *And every open vessel, which hath no covering bound upon it, is unclean*

(Numbers 19:15). In other words, keep your awareness of God and your deep conviction of the eternal verities as a cover, i.e., keep your illumined, conscious mind as a cover over your subconscious, or any old opinions, idle thoughts and false beliefs which will come floating in and take over the powers of your subconscious mind.

Think, speak and act from the standpoint of universal principles and eternal verities rather than from the superimposed structure of fear, ignorance and superstition of the mass mind, sometimes referred to as the race mind, which means the thinking of four and a half billion people. Do your own thinking or the mass mind will do it for you, and as a result, your life will be chaotic.

Taking the Cover Off

The hypnotic operator takes "the cover" (conscious mind) off of the subconscious mind. He gives a suggestion directly to the subconscious, which acts immediately upon the suggestion. It has been demonstrated and proven that even a *post* hypnotic suggestion will be carried out to the consternation of even a recalcitrant hypnotized subject. Time is actually collapsed in experiments of this kind.

What does all this show? Simply that there is a creative medium in your subconscious that responds to the nature of your thought. When you find creativity, you have found God, or the One Power, in essence. God created the universe and all things therein contained. God created you, and the Creative Power is within you. You have freedom to use any power two ways. You have freedom to create sickness or health, failure or success, poverty or wealth by the nature of your habitual thinking and imagery. This is the ancient mystery of good and evil—never quite understood throughout the ages. The Bible points out that Moses drew forth his hand white with leprosy or glowing with health according to the way he used his mind. This applies to all of us.

You Are Adam and Eve

And God said, Let us make man in our image, after our likeness . . . (Genesis 1:26). This means your two natures—conscious and subconscious—bring forth all manifestation and experiences in your lives according to your habitual thinking and imagery. Adam (your conscious mind) and Eve (your subconscious mind) simply represent a portrayal of the interaction between your conscious and subconscious minds. Through these two (male and female) you create always a third—a "son"—your world, your experiences and conditions in life, your demonstrations and all other phases of your life.

Do You Have Free Will?

What are you choosing now? You have choice, volition and initiative. Millions choose old age, lack, limitation, sickness, disease and misfortune of all kinds. All this is a result of man's having surrendered his real heritage (spiritual dominion). Your free will ends when you make the wrong choice such as a belief and faith in outer conditions and effects.

You are here to choose from the Kingdom of God within you. Choose harmony, peace, beauty, Divine love, Divine right action, and Divine law and order, which is Heaven's first law. In other words, choose whatsoever things are noble, Godlike, dignified and wonderful. The fall of man is simply man's failure to choose the beautiful and the good. Millions are held in the chains of bondage to false beliefs, sickness, hate, jealousy and false concepts of a God of love.

You Were Not Born with Fears or Complexes

I explained to an elderly woman during our trip to China that she was not born with any fears, prejudices, religious beliefs or racial taboos; that all these were given to her by parents and others such as relatives, teachers, clergymen, etc. She was full of a fear of death and afterlife and believed she would be punished by some angry God for her past sins.

She began to understand that her mind when she was born was like virgin soil; then the fears, false beliefs about God, life and the universe were impinged on this subconscious mind and left their imprints there. Her racial and religious prejudices were all imparted to her and acquired when she was young and impressionable. She was hungry for the Truth, however, and came to realize that God, or the Life Principle in all of us, is no respecter of persons, does not judge or punish, but that we do hurt and punish ourselves by misuse of the Law and by erroneous and stupid thinking.

At my suggestion she began to read out loud three or four times a day the 27th Psalm, the great antidote to fear; and I observed a tremendous change in her attitude during the rest of the trip. Ofttimes the explanation is the cure.

Original Sin

Man's failure to realize his Divine origin and his sense of separation from the Divine Source, taking the commandments of man for the commandments of God, is original sin—a falling away from and missing the mark of harmony, health, peace and abundance. The Fallen Angel, Fall from Heaven and Lucifer's Fall all mean the same thing—a fall from harmony, peace, beauty and love—a fall from grace.

Heaven means the Invisible Intelligence in which you live, move and have your being. It also means your mind at peace. The old saying is true: "Self-forgiveness is heaven, self-condemnation is hell." Jesus said: *While I was with them in the world, I kept them in thy name: those that thou gavest me I have kept, and none of them is lost, but the son of perdition; that the scripture might be fulfilled* (John 17:12). This means I keep all things *in thy name* by claiming, "I am that thing." You keep all your mental images fixed *in thy name,* meaning that you feel the naturalness of the thing prayed for.

The son of perdition means the belief in loss, and once this belief in loss dies, there is no loss. There is no such thing as a lost soul, for example. No man or thing can be lost in the Infinite. God can't lose Himself. God is the Life of you, the Reality of you. You may be lost temporarily to health, peace, joy or wealth; but you can always go back to the Infinite Source and claim boldly that which you thought you had lost. Nothing is lost in the Infinite.

The Meaning of the Unforgivable Sin

But he that shall blaspheme against the Holy Ghost hath never forgiveness, but is in danger of eternal damnation (Mark 3:29). The Holy Ghost means the Holy Spirit, or God within you. To blaspheme in Biblical terminology is to tell lies about God. To sin means to miss the mark of harmony, health and peace, or failure to reach your goal in life.

You are sinning against the Holy Spirit when you fail to believe in the One Power and ascribe power to outer things instead, thereby living in bondage to false gods. There is no such thing as an unforgivable sin. God, or the Life-Principle, is forever forgiving you, whether you cut your finger, burn yourself or get ill. The Divine Presence always seeks to heal, to restore, and It never punishes.

We punish ourselves by shutting ourselves off from the guidance, love, and healing power of God. When you forgive yourself, you are forgiven. As long as you refuse to accept the Truth appertaining to God, however, and as long as you refuse to forgive yourself, then you are rejecting the Divine influx and the healing power of God. As long as you insist on condemning yourself and feeling guilty, no help or healing can come to you. In that sense only is it unforgivable —while it lasts in you.

All you have to do is to change your attitude. Forgive yourself and the past is forgotten and remembered no more. You must not read the Oriental language of the Bible in a literal sense. For example, the man who was a thief, robbing widows and others, and now is honest, sincere and leading an upright life has forgiven himself and is no longer a thief. He is a new man in God and is transformed. The old man (the thief) is dead and a new man is born. He is no longer the same man spiritually, mentally, psychologically or physically. Science says we have a new body every seven months. The murderer who is now a good man, contributing to society and leading a full and happy life, has forgiven himself; he is a new man in God.

The Operation of Grace

In talking this morning with a widow here in Leisure World, called Laguna Hills, I learned that she had had a malignant tumor, but that her surgeon had told her this morning that an X-ray revealed it had disappeared. She was very happy. A month ago she was worried and upset, and at my suggestion she began to operate the spiritual power of Divine love, which is called Grace. She knew the law of mind, being a former student of the late Ernest Holmes.

She spoke with authority to her body; and for about half an hour three or four times a day, she affirmed boldly and with confidence, "God's love saturates my whole being. God's peace fills my soul, and I give thanks for the miraculous healing taking place now." She adhered regularly to this prayer process; and when fear thoughts came, she supplanted them with the words, "God's love fills my whole being."

This neutralized all the negative thoughts, forming constructive energy, blessing her. She took the pain-killing drug, Codeine, prescribed by her doctor and blessed him regularly. By speaking with authority, she had succeeded in dissolving everything unlike harmony, wholeness and perfection in her body. She played on her body a melody of God.

Spirit and Matter

Modern science today confirms what the ancient Vedas said thousands of years ago: that matter was the lowest degree of Spirit and that Spirit was the highest degree of matter. Einstein said that matter and energy are interconvertible and interchangeable; that matter is energy slowed down to the point of visibility. Energy is a term used by science for Spirit, or God. Basically, Spirit and matter are one. Today we say it is a world of densities, frequencies and intensities. In other words, all is Spirit, and the whole world is Spirit manifesting in multitudinous forms of expression.

The Spirit in you is the real cause of all experience. Matter, in and of itself, has no volition, no initiative. It is not self-acting. It is subject to your mental activity. Your body moves only as it is moved upon. Your body acts as it is acted upon. The body of a man who has gone on to the next dimension does not talk, walk, smile or move. The reason is that the Life-Principle has left him and he is now functioning in higher dimensions of mind. His body undergoes dissolution, which is a natural phenomenon, and becomes grass, hail, and snow. In other words, it returns to its primordial substance.

You must become aware of one cardinal truth: Externals, such as people, conditions, circumstances and the phenomenalistic world, are not causative and do not determine your misery, suffering or happiness. You must begin to inculcate into your cranium that effects are not causative. The cause is always within your own beliefs and attitudes of mind. For example, a man working in the bank learns that there is an epidemic of flu going around and he is full of fear and anxiety that he might get an attack. Some of his associates in the bank are at home ill with the flu. The suggestions from the radio or from others in the office have no creative action. It is his own fear or expectancy. The suggestion, in and of itself, is powerless unless it awakens the creative action of his mind, which is the movement of his own thought. The creative power is in his own mind, and he has the power to reject all negative suggestions.

Recently, in talking with a banker friend of mine who was full of fear that he might catch the flu because others in his office were quite ill at home, I suggested that he affirm frequently, "I am all health. God is my health," realizing that God, or the I AM within him, could not be sick, frustrated, depleted or hurt in any way. Gradually, he seemed to build up an immunity and remained completely free, even though all the other members of his family became ill with the flu.

External conditions, circumstances and suggestions of others are secondary causations only. In order for any external condition to affect you, you must accept the idea or suggestion; then it becomes a movement of your own mind, which is the primary cause. Remember that it is only when a suggestion awakens a response in you that creative action takes place.

She Was Allergic to Red Roses

Recently a woman said to me that she was very allergic to red roses; that they caused paroxysmal attacks, tearing of the lachrymal ducts of the eye and inflammation of the mucosa, creating great difficulty in breathing. She felt that the red roses were the cause. If this were a law, then all those in contact with red roses would be allergic.

However, the truth of the matter was that the man she married had always given her red roses, sending them to her office and home, while courting her. After a few years of marriage, though, he had run off with a younger girl, telling his wife that she was too old for him. She was full of resentment and hatred towards her ex-husband and his girl friend. From that moment on she became allergic to red roses.

Roses have no power to induce attacks of hay fever, asthma or any other respiratory condition. She associated red roses with her ex-husband; and her resentment, antagonism and intense hatred caused the subconscious to bring on these symptoms. Negative, destructive emotions lodged in the subconscious mind cannot have a constructive outlet. Being negative, they must have a destructive effect on the body as well as all phases of life.

Her release came when she began to understand what she was doing to herself and that what is inside the mind causes experiences outside the mind—that thoughts are things. Her attitude and emotions are always projecting themselves into form, expression and condition. She decided to forgive herself for harboring these negative emotions and decided to release her ex-husband and his girl friend to God, wishing for them all the blessings of life. Whenever they came to her mind, she would affirm, "I have released you. God be with you."

After some days she was free in her mind, because there was no longer any sting there. She filled her subconscious with these life-giving truths several times a day: "I live, move and have my being in God. I breathe the pure breath of the Holy Spirit, and my whole being is permeated by the vitalizing life of Spirit. I am now whole and perfect. Praise God, from Whom all blessings flow." She healed herself and is now free.

You Are Not a Slave

Realize that the Spirit within you is omnipotent, supreme and the primal cause. There is nothing to oppose It, thwart It or vitiate It. This inner movement of the Invisible Power to the visible makes you a lord and master in your world. Realize that you were born to have dominion and place all things under your feet (understanding).

A few weeks ago I was speaking at the Unity Church in Phoenix, whose minister is Dr. Blaine Mays. His ministry is going ahead by leaps and bounds. He inspires all his co-workers in a wonderful way, and he is the central figure in the propagation of the New Thought message around the world, since he is the President of the International New Thought Alliance.

I had an appointment with one of his parishioners,

who informed me that for years she had suffered from emphysema, due, she was told, to cigarettes. I gave her a very old prayer, which is lost in the mists of time: "I inhale the peace of God and I exhale the love of God. The breath of the Almighty giveth me life, peace and harmony."

I have recently received a beautiful letter from her, wherein she said that she had used the prayer for about half an hour slowly, quietly and feelingly prior to sleep every night, and that a complete healing had followed. She proved that she was not a victim of matter (physical condition) but the master, a free-born spirit moving triumphantly and victoriously wherever she desired.

The Monk Had the Same Idea

The city of Foshan in China is noted for its restored ancient temple and its famous pottery factory. In talking through an interpreter with one of the monks, he asked me my idea of the Crucifixion. I explained to him the age-old teaching that when the Absolute becomes relative or is made manifest, that is the Crucifixion, the crossing over from the Invisible Presence to the manifest world. That is the first Crucifixion.

He agreed with that. Furthermore, he added that every man portrays the Crucifixion, which, of course, common sense tells you is true. God, the Living Spirit Almighty, is embodied in every man, and each man is crucified on the cross of matter. The monk sp out his arms to the right and left, revealing the real crucifix. It is true that the Divine Spirit (God) is stretched upon a cross of matter, limited by it and controlled by the seeming evidence of the five senses. The average man is not aware that he houses God and that the power of the Almighty is within him. Actually, you are not imprisoned by your body.

Some time ago Professor Hart, an associate of Dr. Rhine of Durham University, wrote an article, "Man Outside His Body," wherein he pointed out that students could leave their bodies, move ponderable objects, and that they had tactile, auditory and visual capacities outside their bodies. Of course, this is not new. Thousands of people all over the world, including the author, have left their physical bodies and appeared to others at a distance. I read some time ago that the Russian secret service had trained certain psychics to leave their bodies and investigate and explore the secret operations of our Defense Department. Again, this is nothing new. You can use any faculty of the mind two ways.

Phineas Parkhurst Quimby was America's greatest healer. He promised a woman one hundred miles away that he would 'visit' her the following Sunday at 7:30. He gave the letter to his son, who forgot to mail it. In Quimby's manuscripts, edited by Horatio Dresser, it points out that at exactly 7:30 p.m. on Sunday Quimby was seen by a guest in the woman's home, who described him in detail, and the lady of the house said, "That is Dr. Quimby. He is treating me."

Quimby said, "I know that I can condense my identity and appear at a distance." He could be in two places at the same time. In other words, his physical body was in Belfast, Maine, and his subtle body, or fourth-dimensional body, was one hundred miles away. The astral body or, as some call it, the spiritual body is a more rarefied, attenuated body capable of going through closed doors and collapsing time and space.

You have all your faculties outside your body, as you are, in reality, a mental and spiritual being, and you will have bodies to infinity. Dr. Quimby was not bound, restricted or circumscribed by a physical body.

The Cosmic Crucifixion

A teacher at the Yoga Forest University, India, stretched forth his arms and said to the students that the Holy Spirit was crucified on a cross of matter and felt confined, but he also said that he was not limited or restricted and was able to teach people at a distance and appear to them whenever he wished. Psychologically speaking, the Crucifixion is the crossing over of your desire to your subconscious mind, where it is fixed or impregnated in the subconscious; and when that takes place, your prayer is answered. Whatever is emotionalized and felt to be true is expressed on the screen of space.

When your prayer is answered, you experience the resurrection. There can't be a resurrection without first experiencing a Crucifixion. This is the basis of all prayer. The words "Crucifixion" and "crossification" mean the same thing. When the sun crossed the equator on March 21, the ancient mystics referred to that phenomenon by saying that the sun had crossified or crucified itself so that man might live. At this time all the seeds frozen in the ground during the long winter sleep are resurrected and the desert rejoices and blossoms as the rose.

The ancient Hebrews referred to the crossing of the sun over the imaginary line called the equator as shedding its blood or life on the Passover. The Passover and the Crucifixion both tell the same story. The only difference is in the words "pass over" and "cross over." Both mean the same thing. Blood in the Bible refers to the giving of life, and the rays of the sun at that season of the year certainly give life to all nature. All scriptures are psychological and spiritual dramatizations of the Truth and reveal their meaning only as they are interpreted psychologically and spiritually.

If you are ill and you mentally and spiritually unite with the ideal of wholeness, vitality and peace of mind and you feel the reality of perfect health, you have crossed over from sickness to health. You are nailed to the ideal of wholeness. Nail in the Bible means your inner feeling, and your conviction of God's wholeness, beauty and perfection. You are nailed or fixed in the belief of perfect health now.

Dictionary of the Sacred Language of All Scriptures and Myths (Gaskell)

The Crucifixion is a very old symbol and represents the death of the archetypal man on the cross of matter, all of which means that the Divine Presence of God is housed in every person in the world. This dictionary also refers to the Crucifixion as another symbol of the Divine Sacrifice, that is, the limitation of the Divine energies and qualities of God within forms of matter. The Crucifixion story was regarded as symbolical of the Divine Spirit (God) involved in matter.

. . . *For it is written, Cursed is every one that hangeth on a tree* (Galatians 3:13). A curse is the negative use of the Law, and when a man is hung on a tree, naturally he can't walk or move around or go anyplace. He has no traction and is actually immobilized. He is a victim of his environment.

This is all symbolic, indicating there are millions of people who feel they are victims of their environment, conditioning, heredity and social surroundings. Man must learn that the Living God is in this tomb of matter which he calls his body and that by uniting with this Presence and Power, he can rise, transcend, grow and lead a full and happy life. Some of our greatest minds came out of the slums and ghettos of the world.

She Said an Angel Saved Her

I received a phone call from a woman who was staying at the MGM Hotel in Las Vegas, where so many people lost their lives, hundreds of others were seriously hurt, and many lost their valuables. This woman had had a vivid dream, wherein a beautiful angelic-like woman had appeared to her, saying, "Leave the hotel at once. There will be a fire and many will die." She followed the instructions and checked out twelve hours before the holocaust. The angel was the Invisible Intelligence of her deeper mind, warning her and revealing what was about to take place.

Your Higher Self always seeks to protect you. Sometimes the answer comes in a dream and a vision of the night. This woman meditates on the 91st Psalm every night of her life.

Special Prayer of Protection

"God is all there is. One with God is a majority. *If God be for me who can be against me?* (Romans 8:31). I know and believe God is the Living Spirit Almighty—the Ever-Living One, the All-Wise One—and there is no power to challenge God. I know and accept completely that when my thoughts are God's thoughts, God's power is with my thoughts of good. I know I cannot receive what I cannot give, and I give out thoughts of love, peace, light and goodwill to this person or persons (mention name or names) and to everyone else. I am immunized and God-intoxicated, and I am always surrounded by the sacred circle of God's love. The whole armor of God surrounds me and enfolds me. I am Divinely guided and directed, and I enter into the joy of living. *In thy presence is fulness of joy; at thy right hand there are pleasures for evermore* (Psalm 16:11)."

CHAPTER 3

Why You Can Be Healed

In the Book of Exodus, Chapter 15:26, we read: . . . *If thou wilt diligently hearken to the voice of the Lord thy God, and wilt do that which is right in his sight, and wilt give ear to his commandments, and keep all his statutes, I will put none of these diseases upon thee, which I have brought upon the Egyptians: for I am the Lord that healeth thee.*

There is only one Healing Presence operating in all animals, in the soil, in the trees, and in all mankind. To heal means to make whole. Disease is a lack of ease, or peace of mind. The tendency of the Life-Principle is to heal, and all healings are spiritual. We are told that we must do that which is lawful and right, and then disease shall not touch us.

The word *Egyptian* in the Bible means thoughts of lack, limitation, darkness and disease; in other words, it is negative thinking. You are what you think all day long. Every thought is creative. Watch your thoughts and make sure that they conform to whatsoever things are true, lovely, noble and Godlike. I AM mentioned in this Bible verse means Being, Life, Awareness, God—the Only Presence and Power.

Another wonderful verse in the Bible dealing with healing reads: *Bless the Lord, O my soul, and forget not all his benefits: Who forgiveth all thine iniquities; who healeth all thy diseases; Who redeemeth thy life from destruction; who crowneth thee with loving-kindness and tender mercies; Who satisfieth thy mouth with good things; so that thy youth is renewed like the eagle's* (Psalm 103:2–5).

In this verse you are adjured to be thankful for all your blessings because the grateful and uplifted heart is always close to God and in tune with the creative forces of the universe. When your mind and heart are lifted up in joyous expectancy, you become a spiritual magnet attracting all kinds of good to yourself. You are also reminded that God, or life, is forever forgiving you; but you must also forgive yourself, and the moment you do that and resolve not to repeat that negation, the past is forgotten and remembered no more. God is love and cannot do anything unloving. The tendency of the Life-Principle is to express Itself as harmony, beauty, joy, love, peace; in other words, it is the Life more abundant.

The soul is your subconscious mind, and whatever the sickness or ailment, it is always due to a group of negative thoughts charged with fear lodged in your subconscious mind. You change your subconscious by prayer, and by prayer we mean the contemplation of the truths of God from the highest standpoint. When you fill your subconscious with the eternal verities and forgive yourself, you will neutralize and obliterate all the negative patterns in your deeper mind; then the embodiment must also disappear. That is the basis of all healing.

How to Preach to Yourself

Jesus said to the disciples: *And as ye go, preach, saying, the kingdom of heaven is at hand. Heal the sick, cleanse the lepers, raise the dead, cast out devils: freely ye have received, freely give* (Matthew 10:7–8). All ill health is actually a lack of wholeness or sense of oneness with the Infinite Healing Presence within everybody. In other words, when we are ill, we are separated from the Source of wholeness, beauty, vitality and perfection.

The Psalmist says, . . . *He leadeth me beside the still waters. He restoreth my soul* . . . (Psalm 23:2–3). The soul is the subconscious mind, and this deeper mind must be restored to wholeness by a new attitude, a new way of thinking and feeling. The body portrays and brings forth whatever is impressed in the subconscious mind.

She Restored Her Soul

A grandmother here in Leisure World was all upset because she had learned that her grandson was living with a girl in Hawaii and neglecting his studies at the

University. She was furious because he had fathered a child out of wedlock. Since she was paying for his tuition, she felt betrayed and hurt.

I explained to her that he was over twenty-one and so was his girl friend and that she could not control his life; furthermore, she was passing judgment on them and condemning them. This was the cause of her very high blood pressure, which drugs did little to reduce to normal.

She began to realize that her attitude was all wrong and that her anger, hostility and resentment were poisonous and destructive emotions which affected her whole being and accomplished nothing. Accordingly, she followed a simple procedure of scientific prayer, as follows: "I release my grandson and his girl friend to God completely. They are Divinely guided. Divine right action governs them. God loves them and cares for them. Divine law and order govern their lives, and they are expressing more and more of God's truth and beauty every day."

She adhered to these truths regularly and they sank down into her subconscious, neutralizing the poison pockets there. Whenever she thought of them, she affirmed, "God is guiding you. God loves you and cares for you." Her blood pressure dropped steadily and her mind is now at peace. She had discovered that there was no one to change but herself. This is spiritual healing.

The Ideal Technique

Attune your mind to the Infinite Healing Presence within you and think from the standpoint of universal principles and eternal verities. Preach to yourself and teach your mind to let go of appearances, false beliefs and negative emotions. Accept mentally and wholeheartedly the great truth that Spirit, or God, or the Infinite Healing Presence is the only Cause; that conditions, processes and forms are effects; and that you do not make an effect a cause. God is Infinite Spirit; there is no other Power or Cause.

She Discovered the Limitless Power

Our newspapers are full of news regarding these devastating fires hitting Southern California and destroying hundreds of homes. I had a call on Thanksgiving Day (1980) from an old friend who has been listening to me for over thirty years on radio, in Los Angeles, and who is now attending my lectures in the Saddleback Valley Plaza Cinema every Sunday at 11:00 a.m. in El Toro. He was all excited and said that he had heard that his home was endangered by the fire; but before he got there, his wife, who had been paralyzed and bedridden for five years, was found walking around outside seeking to find some valuables in the debris.

She had smelled smoke and knew the house was

on fire. The idea to save her life at all costs seized her mind, and the power of the Almighty responded to her focal point of attention. In the emergency situation her conscious mind was thrust aside, permitting the power of the Infinite lodged in her subjective depths to express Itself. The power was always there, but in her conscious mind she assumed and believed she was paralyzed for life. Her subconscious mind accepts no such limitation, for the I AM, or the Infinite Presence and Power, resides in the subconscious mind. There are many such instances in times of emergency, fear and shock.

Faith Healing and Spiritual Healing

Healings take place all over the world. There are healings at Shinto shrines, Buddhistic shrines, and at various other shrines and waters throughout the world. Many are healed by charms, icons, amulets, bones of saints and relics of holy men. Many go to Lourdes and other so-called sacred places. Some bathe in the waters and are healed; others are not. Some go there with great expectancy, faith and fired-up imagination and blind belief, and they get results. Whether the object of your faith be true or false, your subconscious will respond. Many have a false belief that God will suspend His laws and universal principles of healing because of their petition. This, of course, is false. God and His laws remain the same yesterday, today and forever.

WHY YOU CAN BE HEALED

Many get healings by voodoo doctors because of their blind faith or belief. Healings take place at some evangelical meetings where people are emotionally aroused and subject to hypnotic suggestion. The trouble with all these types of healings, however, is that most of them are followed by relapse. The reason is that in order to have a permanent healing, you must eradicate the cause. If you have not eradicated, purified and cleansed your subconscious, the condition reappears.

Spiritual healing is based on the union of your conscious and subconscious mind, scientifically directed, where you claim that what is true of God is true of yourself and the other. Also, you must completely forgive yourself and others, because the Holy Spirit—the Spirit of wholeness—will not flow through a contaminated mind. Before any real or permanent healing can take place, there must come forgiveness, which means to give for; and you give yourself the mood of love, peace, goodwill and confidence in the goodness of God in the land of the living. Wish for everyone what you wish for yourself. You will always know when you have forgiven because you can meet the person or persons in your mind and you no longer sizzle.

When your conscious and subconscious minds are in tune with the Infinite, healing follows. Prayer therapy consists in reconditioning your conscious and subconscious mind. In other words, you reprogram your deeper mind by constantly repeating and reiterating the great eternal truths of life, which belong to all men and women. Teach your own mind to drop all its illusions and weird, grotesque and absurd beliefs about God and His laws and accept the healing power of God operating instantly when you call on It.

The Kingdom of Heaven Is at Hand

The kingdom of harmony, peace, love, joy, abundance and all the riches of the Infinite are within you. Peace is now, claim it; joy is now, claim it; love is now, claim that Divine love fills my soul; power is now, claim that the power of the Almighty is flowing through me now; the answer is now; abundance is now; guidance is now. God is the Eternal Now! You might as well claim these truths now as fifty years from now. Why postpone your good?

Preach to yourself, which means you announce these truths to your assembled thoughts; and when you know the Truth, you can practice it and teach it. You can't give what you don't have. Healing is now. Why wait for it? The Infinite Healing Presence is within you. You must teach yourself first and get rid of all illusions and false concepts and superstitions. Then you will get results.

The disciples are within you. You have twelve powers* and you are here to discipline these twelve

*See *Living Without Strain* by Dr. Joseph Murphy, DeVorss and Co., Inc., Marina del Rey, Ca., 1959.

faculties of mind. Before you can preach or teach others, you must first teach yourself. A man or a woman who has an intense urge to go out and change the world reveals his limitations and lack of understanding by that conviction. It is a great truism that when a person is limited, restricted, he tends to project that limitation on to others. When you listen to television or radio and hear the frightful and absurd teachings, which are a complete distortion of Truth, you realize that these people have not preached the Truth to themselves.

Truth sets you free and does not instill guilt, fear, doubt and limitation in your mind. Truth removes all shackles, all false interpretation of Life, and sets you on the high road to happiness, freedom and peace of mind.

What Do You See in the Other?

Did you ever stop to think that what you see in the other must also be within you? An ancient writer said, "What thou seest, that too become thou must, God if thou seest God, dust if thou seest dust." The world we see is the world we are. We are constantly projecting on to others our imperfections, shortcomings, prejudices and biases. In other words, we are constantly looking out at the world through the content of our own mentality.

It is no use for you to get a mystic wand and decide to transform the world. When you awaken to the truths of Life, you will realize that the world you see is largely a projection of yourself. Begin to see the Presence of God in the other and salute the Divinity in each person. If you want to get along with others in your home or office, make it a habit to affirm frequently, "The Spirit in me speaks to the Spirit of ____________ and there are harmony, peace, love and understanding between us."

Remember, if you want a perfect world, you will never see it perfect until you become perfect yourself. You can't see other than through the contents of your own consciousness. *Unto the pure all things are pure* . . . (Titus 1:15). . . . *There is nothing unclean of itself: but to him that esteemeth any thing to be unclean, to him it is unclean* (Romans 14:14). It was your concept of yourself that caused you to see others as you did.

Change your concept of yourself; claim you are a son or daughter of the Living God, and you will begin to see a different world. If you are identified with the lovely, you can see only the lovely. Your twelve disciples, or twelve faculties, must be disciplined, controlled and directed along Godlike ways. For example, one of your disciples is imagination. Consequently, imagine what is lovely and of good report. Imagine you are doing what you love to do. Feel the reality of it and it will come to pass.

Your vision is what you are looking at in your mind, on what you are focussed, and to what you are giving your attention. What you give attention to will be magnified in your life. If you say, "Okay, I am a failure. I am no good. I am a flop, etc.," this attitude will cause you to fail, to be frustrated, and to become bitter and disappointed. Furthermore, you won't be able to get along with others or to be promoted because of this low estimate of yourself. Affirm boldly, "I am born to win, to succeed. I am a tremendous success, and through the power of God I rise over all obstacles, impediments and difficulties. I am happy, joyous and free."

Keep preaching these truths to your mind. Persist, making it a habit. Through frequent occupancy of your conscious mind, these truths will sink down into your subconscious; and the latter, being compulsive, will compel you to express that with which you impregnated your subconscious. You are announcing to yourself that the kingdom of harmony, peace, abundance and security is here and now. Be careful that you do not subsequently deny what you are affirming.

Your judgment is your conclusion in your mind. In other words, you are always choosing between that which is true and that which is false. Choose harmony, peace, right action, success, abundance, beauty and Divine love. These are principles, and when you dwell on these you activate them and make them potent and functional in your life. Discipline all your faculties according to Divine Truth.

She Heals by Her Presence

A few months ago I had a wonderful conversation with a woman in Tokyo. She belongs to the Seicho-No-Ie Foundation conducted by Dr. Taniguchi. He is sometimes referred to as the Gandhi of Japan. She is a marvelous spiritual healer. She is poised, serene and calm and has a marvelous spiritual vibration. She exudes the healing atmosphere.

She said that when she visits the sick in the hospital, she sits at the bedside and quietly contemplates the healing presence of God saturating the ill person. She remains in that silent attitude for five or ten minutes. Ofttimes there is an automatic healing. She says very little to the patient, just a few words. Her spiritual vibrations enter the subconscious of the patient, restoring his soul.

She pointed out clearly that it is impossible for a spiritually dedicated person who feels a sense of wholeness and oneness with the Infinite to live in a sick body. Paul speaks to us, saying that . . . *the fruit of the Spirit is love, joy, peace, longsuffering, gentleness, goodness, faith, meekness, temperance: against such there is no law* (Galatians 5:22–23).

Claim boldly that you are expressing more of God's love, peace, and harmony every day, and as a result you will find yourself moving onward, upward and Godward. As you saturate your mind with these truths, wholeness and vitality will be generated in all phases of your life. We must understand the Oriental philosophy and not acquire the insane idea that we are placed here to suffer. How could God or Spirit suffer? All of us suffer because of our ignorance and misuse of law. To suffer is to undergo, to bear.

The men who went to the moon suffered setbacks, trials, difficulties and frustrations. They burned the midnight oil, so to speak, to solve their many intricate problems, but they finally achieved victory and triumph. They suffered for the joy that was set before them.

The publisher of one of the books I authored wanted me to change certain chapters, which I did. Six times he wanted the content rearranged, objecting to some passage or other. You might say I suffered from frustration and rejection by even rewriting the theme, but finally it was accepted and the book became a best seller. It is now printed in many foreign languages. The time it took me to replace the old and supplant it with the new could be called longsuffering, all of which means you bear the load or inconvenience long enough to make the change.

The alcoholic suffers or bears the shakes and the jitters for a time until he succeeds in supplanting his destructive habit with peace, harmony and sobriety. In other words, he undergoes some pain or frustration temporarily for the joy of freedom, peace of mind and sobriety. This attitude is creative, ennobling and blessing him. He has replaced the craving for alcohol and is enjoying the fruit of the Holy Spirit.

This is a constructive attitude of mind. It should be repeated here that to think that suffering is the will of God is a form of insanity and gross stupidity.

He Could Not Be Healed

Some years ago I visited a sick man in his home. The doctor said that there was no reason why he should not be healed and go back to work. During my conversation with him, I learned that he was a born-again Christian, that he tithed to his church, followed the Ten Commandments, visited the sick, went to church and took communion regularly; therefore, why should God do this to him? He railed at God and was angry that he was sick, and losing money and business. He was petulant, crotchety and cantankerous and announced that he would give up his religion, as God did not play fair with him.

All this is folderol and balderdash. I explained to him that he would never get a healing with that attitude of mind, because destructive emotions were behind his illness, and that he was prolonging his misery by denouncing God and his sickness. I suggested that he give thanks for the doctor and the nurse who visited him, should follow their instructions and bless them, and then forgive himself for harboring these negative thoughts. I further suggested that he frequently give thanks for his miraculous healing with these words: "Father, I thank thee for thy marvelous healing taking place now. I know God in the midst of me is mighty to heal."

He followed that advice and he discovered that his changed attitude had changed everything. He realized that there was no one to blame but himself. As a result, he had a wonderful recovery in a few weeks. When he healed his mind, his body was healed likewise.

Blessed Are the Meek

In the fifth chapter of Matthew, verse 5, we read: *Blessed are the meek: for they shall inherit the earth.* This does not mean that you should feel that you are a worm in the dust. If you do, everybody is going to step on you. Earth means manifestation, your body, home, business, social status and all phases of your life. To inherit the earth means you have dominion over all your external conditions.

In Biblical language the word "meek" refers to teachability and open-mindedness, faith in God and all things good. This is the key to success. Free your mind from stubbornness and the stiff-necked attitude of mind and let in the sunshine of God's love. When you pray, relax, let go and free your mind from all resentment, pugnacity and ill will and wish for everyone all the blessings of life. What you wish for others comes into your own experiences.

By Grace Ye Are Saved

. . . *By grace ye are saved* (Ephesians 2:5). The grace of God is the wisdom and love of God operating in your mind and body and in all phases of your life.

A young man who had hurt himself in a game and who had considerable trouble walking began to affirm, "God walks in me. It is God walking in me now." At my suggestion he kept repeating this over and over again, knowing that sooner or later it would enter his subconscious mind* and come to pass. The Bible says, *Draw nigh to God, and he will draw nigh to you* . . . (James 4:8). In other words, as you turn to the Infinite Spirit, It will turn to you, and by the law of reciprocal relationship, there will be a response in accordance with your prayer of faith and confidence.

This young man persisted, and today he walks perfectly. He discovered the grace of God, which means he discovered the Infinite Healing Presence, Which responded to his habitual thinking and imagery. God is forever seeking expression through you. God is the giver and the gift, and all things have been proffered to you from the foundations of time. Learn to be a good receiver. It is normal and natural for you to be happy, healthy, joyous and prosperous.

Temperance means that you are leading a balanced life, not a lopsided one. You are living in a spiritual and a material world. You must balance both and avoid extremes. You can't live without peace, harmony, joy, love and goodwill. This is the bread or nourishment of heaven. You need inspiration and a transfusion of God's grace. You also need to express

*See *The Power of Your Subconscious Mind* by Dr. Joseph Murphy, Prentice-Hall, Inc., Englewood Cliffs, N.J., 1963.

yourself at your highest level and contribute to humanity your skills, your ability and your talents. The more you give in love and goodwill, the more you have.

She Asked Me to Cast Out the Devil

I am continuously receiving letters from all parts of the world. Some writers are convinced they are possessed by devils which curse them and say all manner of evil to them, using obscenities and profanities and telling them to commit suicide, etc. I find in all such instances that they have gone into their subconscious with hatred, envy, hostility and vengeance. These are the devils which bedevil them; the enemies are of their own household, created by themselves and playing havoc with them. The voices they hear are of their own subconscious mind, which is actually talking back to them based on what they have impressed upon it.

My prescription to them is to forgive themselves for harboring these negative thoughts and to read the 91st Psalm out loud three times slowly four or five times a day and prior to sleep. After each three recitals of the Psalm, they are to sit quietly and affirm silently and quietly, "God's love and God's peace fill my soul," for ten or fifteen minutes. Love dissolves everything unlike itself. When God's love fills the soul, all negation flees before it. God's love is a consuming fire and burns up all negation. The mind is then at peace. You will then speak in a new tongue of faith, confidence, love and goodwill. You will speak in the tongue of a mind at peace and not express a lot of gibberish.

I have seen men take up live serpents and scorpions and place them around their necks. They translate the serpent back to Spirit and are trained to see the Presence of God in all creatures. It is very dangerous and deadly for those who are not conditioned and trained spiritually, as many times in their blind faith in taking the Bible literally, they get bitten and die. You do not tempt the Lord your God.

There is the inner serpent of envy, jealousy and guilt which bites and corrodes the soul. Jealousy is the green-eyed monster, and when it stings your soul, it is real venom, one of the most destructive of all emotions. It is a real poison, and the answer is to fill your mind with age-old truths such as, "Divine love guides me. God loves me and cares for me. The light of God watches over me. I am illumined. I am suffused and submerged in the radiance of the Light Limitless."

Make a habit of this by frequent reiteration in your mind, and you will find that God will wipe away all tears from your eyes and guide you to green pastures and beside still waters.

Psalm of Protection
(Psalm 91)

He that dwelleth in the secret place of the most High shall abide under the shadow of the Almighty.

WHY YOU CAN BE HEALED

I will say of the Lord, He is my refuge and my fortress: my God; in him will I trust.

Surely he shall deliver thee from the snare of the fowler, and from the noisome pestilence.

He shall cover thee with his feathers, and under his wings shalt thou trust: his truth shall be thy shield and buckler.

Thou shalt not be afraid for the terror by night; nor for the arrow that flieth by day;

Nor for the pestilence that walketh in darkness; nor for the destruction that wasteth at noonday.

A thousand shall fall at thy side, and ten thousand at thy right hand; but it shall not come nigh thee.

Only with thine eyes shalt thou behold and see the reward of the wicked.

Because thou hast made the Lord, which is my refuge, even the most High, thy habitation;

There shall no evil befall thee, neither shall any plague come nigh thy dwelling.

For he shall give his angels charge over thee, to keep thee in all thy ways.

They shall bear thee up in their hands, lest thou dash thy foot against a stone.

Thou shalt tread upon the lion and adder: the young lion and the dragon shalt thou trample under feet.

Because he hath set his love upon me, therefore will I deliver him: I will set him on high, because he hath known my name.

He shall call upon me, and I will answer him: I will be with him in trouble; I will deliver him, and honour him.

With long life will I satisfy him, and shew him my salvation.

F. L. Rawson, noted engineer, gives account of a British regiment under the command of Col. Whittlesey, which served in World War I for more than four years without losing a man. This unparalleled record was made possible by means of active cooperation of officers and men in memorizing and repeating regularly the words of the 91st Psalm, which has been called the Psalm of Protection.

CHAPTER 4

The Power of Ideas

Have you ever said, "He bores me"? If so, it is an unconscious confession of guilt within yourself, indicating that you are all wrapped up in yourself and looking for someone to lift you out of your despondency or "self-centeredness." Every time you meet another person, stir up the gift of God within you and say to yourself, "I behold the Presence of God in the other, and I know that at this moment there is a rearrangement of the mental and emotional factors in both of us whereby we blend harmoniously, peacefully, and lovingly." Thoughts are things, and whatever we think about another we are thinking about ourselves.

As a Man Thinketh in His Heart So Is He

For as he thinketh in his heart, so is he . . . (Proverbs 23:7). Many people cite this Biblical quotation from the Book of Proverbs but do not really recognize the tremendous significance of such a profound truth. The heart (in the Bible) means your subconscious mind. Whatever idea you have that is emotionalized or felt as true will be made manifest in your life. Whatever you give attention to and feel to be true will be impressed in your subconscious and brought to pass.

If, for example, you affirm with emphasis and feeling that you will always be poor, can't get ahead in life, that you will be discriminated against and can't do anything about it, you can rest assured that you will get the results decreed by yourself. Likewise, the inverse is true. Claim feelingly and knowingly that you are born to win and to triumph, and that it is your Divine right to be healthy, wealthy, and successful, and that God wants you to be happy, joyous and free. Claim boldly that Divine right action is mine, Divine law and order are mine, and Divine harmony is mine. Declare that God's riches are mine and I am expressing more and more of my Divinity every day. Affirm these truths with feeling and understanding and your subconscious will compel you to express these in your life as experiences, conditions and events.

Your Focused Thought Takes Form

Some years ago Dr. Charles Littlefield, a scientist, discovered the truth of the Biblical quotation, *for as he thinketh in his heart, so is he.* While concentrating his thought on a saline solution by peering through a microscope, he discovered his focused thought took form. One day he concentrated his attention on a frail, elderly lady. He stood gazing intently at her for some time. When he turned back to look at the saline solution, he was surprised to find there a miniature form of this woman. Day after day he concentrated on certain mental pictures, and he was amazed to see his mental imagery take form in the shapes developed by the crystals in the saline solution under the microscope.

Man is what he thinks all day long. Our thoughts are the tools and instruments which fashion, mold and shape our destiny. Your thoughts can be photographed. They have form, shape and structure in your brain now, and are gradually being condensed into muscle, skin, and cells, as well as into experiences, events and conditions.

For many years there has been a revolution going on in the field of chemistry and physics. For example, the postulate of immutable elements is gone; this dogma vanished with the discovery of radioactivity. Scientists today point out that we are living in a dynamic, evolving, changing universe. The late Robert Andrew Millikin, who was head of the California Institute of Technology at Pasadena for many years, said that the two fundamental principles, conservation of mass and conservation of energy, are now gone as distinct and separable verities.

Einstein and other scientists have also pointed out the interconvertibility of energy into mass and mass into energy. Energy and mass are actually one and the same thing operating at different levels of vibration. Matter is energy reduced to the point of visibility. The conception of the conservation of energy and the conservation of mass is considered no longer sacrosanct.

Your body is plastic, porous and pliable. It consists of waves of light existing at different rates of vibration. Modern science teaches that the only difference between one substance and another is the number and rate of motion of the electrons revolving around a nucleus, proving the dictum of Pythagoras that the world is ruled by number and motion.

You Are Dealing with the Invisible

You cannot measure love with a slide rule; neither can you measure peace, happiness, wisdom or understanding. We are dealing with the intangible, the invisible, the imponderable. You cannot see the power that moves your finger to write, nor do you see the power that lifts the chair or table. Your body moves as it is moved upon. Your body acts as it is acted upon. Your body is basically characterized by inertia, and your thoughts, emotions, and imagery are played upon it for good or ill. You can play a melody of God on the tissues of your body or a song of hatred or ill will.

Science and Religion

Professor Jack Holland of San Jose University speaks of science and religion as the two sisters. People must not assert as true what every high school boy knows is false. There are many people in the religious field who believe and teach that the world was made in six days and that God somehow got tired and rested on the seventh day. Geologists, paleontologists, archaeologists, anthropologists, physicists, astronomers and other scientists, however, realize that the cosmos took form according to a definite cosmic design and took countless billions of years to assume the form it now has. All these changes took place in Divine order and sequence according to an archetypal design of the Infinite Intelligence, Which is the only creative power.

The Creative Process

Judge Thomas Troward, author of many inimitable books on mental science, such as the *Edinburgh Lectures, Doré Lectures,* and others, perceived the creative process intuitively, as follows: "The physical history of our planet shows us first an incandescent nebula dispersed over vast infinitudes of space; later it condenses into a central sun surrounded by a family of glowing planets hardly yet consolidated from the plastic primordial matter; then succeed untold millenniums of slow geological formation; an earth peopled by the lowest form of life, whether vegetable or animal; from which crude beginnings a majestic, unceasing, unhurried, forward movement brings things stage by stage to the conditions in which we know them now.''

Six Days of Creation

Look at the six days of creation as six great stages in the evolution of the cosmos. The six days in Genesis have an inner meaning which portrays the six steps in prayer followed by the seventh day, or sabbath, in which you reach the point of conviction or inner knowing that your prayer is answered. In psychological parlance, the six days represent the length of time it takes you to impress or convey your idea or concept in your subconscious mind. As soon as you succeed in impregnating the subconscious by imagining the reality of your desire and feeling the thrill of fulfillment, you have succeeded in impressing the subconscious. Impregnation has taken place. The work of the six days is finished, followed by a period of inner rest called the sabbath, or seventh day, which is the interval of time between the impregnation and its manifestation.

The Value of True Ideals

The most wonderful and valuable form of wealth is a good idea. The Magna Carta was an idea in the mind of man, as was the Declaration of Independence. Ideas move men and nations and inspire men and women to the heights of accomplishment and achievement. An idea is a thought, a mental conception, an image in the mind, an intention.

When you stop to think, you begin to realize that all the great inventions in the world started as an idea in the mind of man. Look around you in Los Angeles, New York or any city, and you will perceive that all the major skyscrapers, major plants and industries, all the great institutions and organizations began as a simple idea. In fact, everything you look at in this world came out of the mind of man, or the mind of God. The universe, the galaxies in space and the billions of stars and suns and worlds came out of the mind of God. The ancient Vedas said, "God thinks and worlds appear." Man thinks and his world appears. What the world needs are lofty, noble, God-like ideas which heal, bless and inspire mankind.

One of the old writers on the laws of mind, Prentice Mulford, said, "Truth heals; lies breed disease." For example, a man is told that he can't walk again due to an accident. He believes it and remains incapacitated. Another man who is hurt even worse than the first is told by a spiritual counsellor that through the power of the Infinite Spirit within him, he can walk again and be healed. His mind is stirred with faith and confidence, and he imagines himself doing all the things he would do were he whole and perfect. His mental image, being backed up by faith and expectancy in the God-Power within him, creates a wonderful demonstration and he is completely healed.

This is the power of a transcendent idea lodged in the mind of man.

Phineas Parkhurst Quimby, who was America's greatest spiritual healer, began healing people of all manner of diseases in the year 1847. He possessed tremendous mental power and concentration and perceived intuitively the inner meaning of the Bible. He used to explain the inner meaning to his very sick patients, because in many instances their maladies were due to false religious beliefs based on the literal interpretation of Scripture. When people had lost all hope and could not be healed by any orthodox procedure, they came to Quimby as a last resort, and he healed them all. He duplicated most of the so-called miracles of the Bible, and if he had lived long enough he would undoubtedly have duplicated all of them.

Quimby said: "I have no doubt that I can go to an audience of a thousand and cure more persons in one lecture than can be cured by all the doctors in the State of Maine in the same time." He was a man of tremendous faith in the Infinite Healing Presence, Which is the only healing power.

What Kind of Ideas Control Your Mind?

All of us tend to be influenced every day by the propaganda of all sorts of news which tend to depress, excite and instill fear into the mind. You must learn to reject all these negative suggestions and supplant them with Godlike ideas which will raise your spirit.

The false predictions of doom and gloom can influence you negatively and cause great trouble. Permit the truths of God to guide you to ways of pleasantness and paths of peace.

Fear and ignorance are rampant today, and if you permit these suggestions to enter your mind, you will develop what is called by psychologists an anxiety neurosis. Insist on governing your mind with true ideas, for then your talents and abilities are encouraged and you become imbued with the confidence and faith that lead you along the path of success and inner peace.

Are There Two Influences Governing You?

All of us are amenable to suggestions, both good and bad. For example, all of us are immersed in the mass mind—that great psychic sea in which all of us are submerged. The race mind, or the mass mind, is the habitual thinking of four and a half billion people on this planet. You know very well that the influence of the mass mind is extremely limiting, causing those influenced by it to be full of fear, ignorance, and superstition. It is very depressing and full of jealousy, envy, greed, and is debilitating in every way.

This means that if you do not do your own thinking, the mass mind will do it for you, because subjectively we are all one and we are telepathically communicating at all times. When you keep prayed up, you neutralize most of this negative influence, as there is no room in your mind then for these morbid, depressive thoughts. Let the God-Presence in you arise and influence you along all lines. This Divine Presence tells you that you are here to conquer, to express yourself at the highest level, and that you are born to win, to succeed, and to lead a full and happy life. These are the influences of the Spirit within you that is always saying to you: Rise, transcend and grow. Move onward and upward. That is the voice of the Divine in you. Let that be your major influence. Cease being a slave to the false beliefs of the world.

The Truth Sets You Free

In the Book of Matthew it is written: *And he entered into a ship, and passed over, and came into his own city. And, behold, they brought to him a man sick of the palsy, lying on a bed: and Jesus seeing their faith said unto the sick of the palsy; Son, be of good cheer; thy sins be forgiven thee. And, behold, certain of the scribes said within themselves, This man blasphemeth. And Jesus knowing their thoughts said, Wherefore think ye evil in your hearts? For whether is easier, to say, Thy sins be forgiven thee; or to say, Arise, and walk?* (Matthew 9:1–5).

The first thing you have to realize when you read the Bible is that it is a psychological and spiritual drama taking place in the consciousness of man. All the characters portrayed represent states of mind in each person. The ship spoken of in the first verse simply means that a ship leaves port to reach its destination. Likewise, each person is a ship travelling from a problem to a solution.

Every person has a goal, and he must leave his present limited state of mind and move forward in faith and confidence to his new goal in life. If you want to go to San Francisco from Los Angeles, you must leave Los Angeles. Likewise, if you want a healing of mind and body, you must leave your old grudges, peeves and resentments in order to get a healing, or an answer to your prayer.

The city mentioned in the first verse is your own mind, and the people who dwell there are thoughts, ideas, beliefs and opinions of all kinds. The true city is one where your mind is in tune with the Infinite Presence within you, which is your Higher Self. Jesus is not only a man in the Bible. He is also a personification of Truth, your own self-confidence that goes into your own temple and announces that with God all things are possible.

These stories in the Bible illustrate the power of God residing in all of us and they urge us to take hold of this power and heal ourselves of all infirmities. This man was lying down in the bed of his mind, believing that he could not be healed. He was actually lying down, however, in a bed of inadequacy and weakness, as well as ignorance.

Jesus, seeing his faith, said to the sick man: *Son,*

be of good cheer; thy sins be forgiven thee. To sin is to miss the mark. You are sinning when you fail to lead a full and happy life. You forgive yourself for being sick when you claim, feel, know and believe that the healing power of God will heal you, and now you become healed. To forgive is to "give for." You have given yourself the pattern of wholeness, vitality and peace of mind for the sick state. Likewise, the man who was a thief and who is now leading an upright, honest life and contributing constructively to humanity has forgiven himself.

This man mentioned in the Bible was undoubtedly lying down in the bed of fear and incurability, refusing to believe he could walk again. Undoubtedly you know many people who were crippled and who now walk uprightly with poise and confidence. There are many people lying down in the bed of their mind, though, saying to themselves that they are unworthy, that they are destined to be poor, that the good things in life are not for them, that it is too good to be true, and that nothing good can happen to them.

All this is tragic, because it is done unto them as they believe. Their subconscious mind responds according to their belief. When they accept in their mind that there is nothing too good to be true, nothing too wonderful to last, for the love and the light and the glory of God are the same yesterday, today and tomorrow, they rise up and walk uprightly in the law and experience the good things of life.

She Walked and Ran

In a recent visit to Las Vegas, I talked with an old friend who told me about his relative who was on crutches and who had been staying a few days at the MGM Hotel in Las Vegas. Her young daughter was with her. The purpose of their stay was to see a medical specialist for the daughter's condition as well as that of herself.

The fire broke out that all of you have read about. The mother smelled the smoke. The young daughter was asleep. The mother threw her crutches away, put the little girl on her back and ran toward the exit and escaped. She is still walking today. She was completely healed. The idea to save her life and that of her little girl seized her mind, and all the power of the Godhead flowed to that focal point of attention.

The Healing Power had always been there, but she had been lying down in the bed of her mind saying to herself: "I'm on crutches; I can't walk." It is well known in the annals of medicine that during emergencies, shock and great fear, people often perform extraordinary feats of heroism, healings take place, some even go through fire and are not burned. In wartime also, many people are seized with a high motivation and great fervor, and when lifted up in consciousness, they feel glorified. Though bullets are whizzing all around them, they are immune and fearless and perform extraordinary acts of heroism.

The Whole World Believes a Lie

Quimby, of whom we spoke earlier in this chapter, said that "the whole world believes a lie, and when I tell it the truth, it thinks the truth is a lie." Millions are brought up in the belief that it is the will of God that they suffer, that externals are causative, that the night air will give them a cold, if they get wet they might catch pneumonia, or that when they grew old their vision, hearing and other faculties will weaken. Millions believe in evil entities, demons and voodooism, and black magic.

The scientific thinker does not give power to the phenomenalistic world. It is an effect, not a cause. The Supreme Power, I AM, is within you. There is nothing to oppose It, challenge It, thwart It or vitiate It. Otherwise, the word omnipotence would have no meaning. The propaganda of fear regarding cancer, the flu and other diseases has no power to disturb you. These are suggestions only and have no power unless they awaken a response within your own mind, which is the creative power of your own mind. Always remember that a suggestion has no power to create the thing it suggests. If someone suggests to you that you will get the flu, you can affirm boldly, "I am all health. God is my health." In that way you neutralize the suggestion and build up an immunity to all disease.

Some say, "Roses give me hay fever." If that were really true, then all people throughout the world would get hay fever when in contact with roses. There are no exceptions to a law. It is obvious that the person who is allergic to roses has made a law for himself. Roses have no such power. The cause is in the subconscious of the person. He may be allergic to his wife or to the fellow next to him on the workbench. It is the things inside the mind that cause the things outside the mind. The inside is always the cause; the outside is the effect of the inner contents of the mind.

His Hand Was Shaking Constantly

A man living here in Leisure World, Laguna Hills, where I live, told me that for several years his right hand had been constantly shaking, actually trembling; it seemed to be full of tremors. He had been told it was due to a nerve in his hand that had been injured. He went to a woman who was noted for spiritual healing, and she gave him a prayer to use frequently. She told him point blank that if he continued using the prayer he would be healed. He had the prayer in his billfold, which read as follows: "God has not given me the spirit of fear but the spirit of power, and of love, and of a sound mind. My faith is in the healing power of God, which created me. I am relaxed and at peace. All my nerves are God's ideas, and I am vitalized, energized, and healed through and through. I give thanks to God!"

He saturated his mind with these simple truths and had a wonderful healing of the palsy. He turned to the Divine man (his Higher Self) within him, and as he called upon the Presence, It responded to him. This is wisdom in action. Wisdom is an awareness of the Presence and Power of God within you, Which responds when you call upon It.

Acquaint Yourself with Him

The Bible says, *Acquaint now thyself with him, and be at peace: thereby good shall come unto thee* (Job 22:21). God indwells you, walks and talks in you. This Presence takes care of you when you are sound asleep. It is the very Life of you. You don't look up in the sky; contact is made within by your own thought. It is the Living Spirit within you, Which created you and gave you the whole world. Boundless love is within you; absolute harmony and infinite intelligence are there waiting for you to call upon all the attributes, potencies and qualities of God. Its nature is to respond to you, and you are told in the 91st Psalm: *He shall call upon me, and I will answer him: I will be with him in trouble; I will deliver him, and honour him* (Psalm 91:15).

Thoughts of Loved Ones

If you have been struggling with thoughts of fear, worry or anxiety about your loved ones, let go of them. Affirm frequently: "I turn (mention their names) __________ over to God completely. I know and believe that God's love, peace and harmony surround them and watch over them. The Spirit of the Lord God watches over them at all times and keeps them in perfect safety. God's healing love is guarding, protecting, inspiring and guiding them in all ways." A prayer such as this will free your mind from anxiety and worry and at the same time will bless and protect your loved ones.

Rising Above the Vexing Situation

Recently I talked with a woman over the phone, who said that she was ready to explode. She said that her husband was afflicted with a fatal illness, that he would not take his medicine, and that he kept humming the same song all day long while sitting in a rocking chair and rocking continuously for hours on end. She said that she was turning to drink and that she had lost her buoyancy and resiliency altogether. She told me that she yells at him, saying, "For heaven's sake, stop it! You're driving me crazy!"

I suggested to her to sit down quietly and do what the Psalmist said. "*I will lift up mine eyes unto the hills, from whence cometh my help* (Psalm 121:1). God gives me peace. God gives me joy, and God loves my husband and cares for him." She began to affirm these truths, actually singing the words. She climbed the mountain and rose above it. The hills mentioned by the Psalmist represent the great truths of God, which heal, invigorate and bring peace to the troubled mind. She discovered then that the constant rocking had no further effect upon her. You can always climb the hills of God and find peace in this changing world.

The Holy Man
(Adapted from The Holy Shadow)

"Long, long ago, there lived a Holy Man so good that the astonished angels came from heaven to see how one could be so godly. He simply went about his daily life radiating love as the star diffuses light and the flowers perfume without even being aware of it. Two words summed up his day: He gave, and he forgave. Yet these words never fell from his lips; they were expressed in his ready smile, his kindness, love, and goodwill.

"The angels said to God, 'Oh Lord, grant him the gift of miracles!'

"God replied, 'I consent; ask what he wishes.'

" 'What do you desire then?' cried the angels.

" 'What can I wish for?' asked the Holy Man, smiling. 'That God give me His grace, with that should I not have everything?'

"The angels insisted, 'You must ask for a miracle, or one will be forced upon you.'

" 'Very well,' said the Holy Man, 'that I may do a great deal of good without ever knowing it.'

"The angels were greatly perplexed. They took counsel together and resolved upon the following plan: Every time the Holy Man's shadow should fall behind him, or at either side, so that he could not see it, it should have the power to cure disease, soothe pain, and comfort sorrow.

"And so it came to pass. When the Holy Man walked along, his shadow on the ground, on either side or behind him, made arid paths green, caused withered plants to bloom, gave clear water to dried-up brooks, fresh color to pale little children, and joy to unhappy mothers. The Holy Man simply went about his daily life pouring forth love as the star diffuses light and the flower perfume without ever being aware of it.

"And the people, respecting his humility, followed him silently, never speaking about his miracles. Little by little, they came even to forget his name, and called him only, 'The Holy Man.' "

CHAPTER 5

The Road to Serenity

You often hear people today saying, "I'm so worried." Many times they do not realize the implications of what they are saying, because every time one says, "I'm so worried," the speaker is making grooves in his subconscious mind. The latter being the seat of habit, the speaker becomes a chronic worrier. For example, the mother worries about her son or daughter, the father worries about the stock market, the salesman about his job, and millions worry about the country, their health and prosperity.

In talking with chronic worriers, I have found that it is not heavy burdens or great tragedies that irritate and upset them, but petty things and insignificant problems. These are . . . *the little foxes that spoil the vines* . . . (Song of Solomon 2:15). Medical men today know that chronic worry undermines the digestion, brings on ulcers and debilitates the entire system. Most worries are inconsequential trifles that fritter away your vital forces.

It Hasn't Happened Yet

The nature of most of our worries is that it is about something that has not happened yet. Look back on your life and you will find that most of the things you worried about never happened, but at the same time you robbed yourself of peace, harmony, vitality and perhaps even made yourself a physical and mental wreck.

What Is Worry?

Worry is faith in the wrong thing. Faith is living in the joyous expectancy of the best, and worry is expecting the opposite. Worry is a focussing of attention on a negative idea to the exclusion of others. Worry could be looked upon as an obsession, which means that you permit a false idea to dominate your mind. You are held in a sort of a hypnotic spell, all self-imposed. In other words, you have a "fixation," which is simply a negative auto-suggestion given to your subconscious mind. A fancy name for chronic worry is compulsive neurosis, which means that you are chewing constantly on some negative aspect, like a dog gnaws at a bone, and sometimes the worrier actually resents being told to change his or her attitude to a constructive viewpoint.

Worried About an Earthquake

An elderly woman living here in Leisure World, Laguna Hills, came to see me with all sorts of statistics about earthquakes all over the world and some predictions by psychics regarding possible earthquakes in California. She seemed to be obsessed with the idea of earthquakes. She was of French origin, so I asked her if she had not heard the phrase *laissez-faire,* which means non-interference, unconcern, philosophic indifference.

I explained to her that most of the predictions by psychics in books and newspapers never happen and that all she had to do was to look at the recent election of President Reagan. Nearly all of the psychics were wrong, wrong, wrong. Paul said, . . . *Whether there be prophecies, they shall fail* . . . (I Corinthians 13:8). Her faith had gone wild, yet she was a profound student of the works of Unity and Science of Mind.

It dawned on her what she was doing to herself. Her blood pressure had become abnormally high and she was a victim of insomnia. Her physician, Dr. Frank Wm. Varese, who practices wholistic medicine, told her to go back to the Psalms, such as the 27th and 91st. I told her that she was looking for trouble, running out to meet it all day long, yet it never arrives. Moreover, other scientists say that there is no sign of an earthquake.

Faith in God and all things good destroys worry and fear. A changed attitude changes everything. I suggested that she give her attention to the great eternal Truths of life, which she was to affirm boldly and feelingly several times a day. In that manner, she would supplant her worry with faith in God and all things good: "I am surrounded by an envelope of God's love. I am invulnerable and nothing can touch me but that which is good and very good. I clothe myself with the garment of Infinite love and Infinite peace. God watches over me, and where I am God is. The whole armor of God surrounds me and I bear a charmed life. Whenever fear or worry comes to my mind, I will immediately affirm, 'God watches over me.' It is wonderful!"

Making a habit of this prayer brought results. She is now practicing *laissez-faire* in her attitude toward events over which she exercises no control.

It Is Not What Happens to Us

I talked with a man recently who had missed a plane. He had a very important contract to sign at the city for which he was headed. His particular flight was cancelled, and he said to himself, "Infinite Spirit has a far better way of handling this contract. It is God in action." He remained poised, serene and calm and took the next flight out, after explaining by phone the situation to those he was to meet.

Everything worked in Divine order for him. You can see that it isn't what happened to him that mattered, it was his thought about it. He had the right attitude. Another man next to him in line at the airport had been very abusive to the clerk, and was obviously agitated and disturbed. He was in what is called an emotional stew, which undoubtedly was destructive to his entire system. All this man really had to do though was to accept the situation and affirm, "I am serene and calm and realize, like Paul, . . . *None of these things move me* . . ." (The Acts 20:24).

Psychosomatic physicians today point out that anger, rage, resentment and frustration cause adrenalin-type hormones to be generated, which, in turn, bring on high blood pressure and an abnormal pulse rate. You can always choose how you are going to react to a certain situation. Remember, all reactions take place in your mind. You have control over your thoughts. You are the boss, and you can order your thoughts along constructive, spiritual lines. You can begin now, today. Affirm frequently: "I am unmoved, undisturbed. I am relaxed and at peace." Decree it, mean it and be sincere, and your subconscious will accept it.

Mental Hunchbacks

There are a great number of people who are what might be termed mental hunchbacks. They feel insecure, inadequate and frustrated. Usually they are down on themselves and suffering from self-criticism and self-condemnation. Their tendency is to project their shortcomings on to others.

You can easily reject their statements and attitudes. You understand their problem: bless them and walk on. This ancient prayer will solve many problems for you: "God grant me the serenity to accept the things

I cannot change, courage to change the things I can, and wisdom to know the difference."

Drifting at Fifty

A lady said to me that she was unhappy, frustrated, had gone through three divorces, was fifty years of age, had written many articles and is in demand as a speaker before women's clubs, but none of her writings had been published. She added, "Maybe a jinx is following me, but in any case I know something is wrong with me." This was the essence of her conversation.

I suggested that it is far more important for her to give up her abnormal fear of evil powers working against her and that it would be far more wonderful and interesting for her to enter a life of goodness and fulfillment. All she had to do then to improve the situation was to direct her attention to that which is good, constructive, harmonious and prosperous, ignoring all the rest.

Accordingly, she performed an experiment for a month, at which time she was to report the results. She deliberately turned her attention to the desirable elements in her life, claiming: "Infinite Intelligence opens up the way for my writings to be accepted. I am happily married, I am Divinely active, I am Divinely compensated. I have a marvelous income consistent with integrity and honesty. I am giving of my talents in a wonderful way. I am appreciated, I am wanted, and I am needed. It is wonderful!"

She adhered regularly to these great affirmatives, redirecting her attention on the constructive side of life. Before the month was over, she advised me that out of the blue sky, recognition came. She was invited to be an assistant to a publisher, and her writings shortly thereafter were all published. Many people became cooperative chiefly on account of her changed attitude. Formerly, she said, they would not have endured her.

She is no longer possessed by limitation, but instead the idea of abundance rules and governs her mind. She is happily married. The enthusiast is a person who is first possessed by a dream, an ideal, and then after a while the dream possesses the person, who is no longer governed by the past.

There is an old poem that illustrates what we have been talking about:

> Mind is the master power that molds and makes
> And man is mind, and ever more he takes
> The tools of thought, and shaping what he will,
> Brings forth a thousand joys, a thousand ills.
> He thinks in secret and it comes to pass,
> Environment is but his looking glass.

Her Psychic Pain

A well-educated woman working in a very prestigious office complained that she was very upset, troubled and annoyed by the frightful, immoral lives her co-workers seemed to be leading. Some of the girls were married and had extra boy friends. The married men had mistresses and openly flaunted their infidelity. This woman felt very self-righteous. She was the sanctimonious type, sometimes referred to as being disgustingly holy.

I explained to her that she does not control the lives of her associates, and if some of them had cancer I'm sure she would not be upset and worried, but compassionate. Or, if some of them had tuberculosis or were crippled or lame, undoubtedly she would want for them health and happiness. Some people have twisted and distorted minds, and the only thing for her to do in that case was to overcome her condemnation of them and pray for them. In that way she would overcome her anger and hostility. Marcus Aurelius said, "Where there is no judgment, there is no pain."

She was to cease passing judgment on them, because whatever bitter thoughts she had about them were created in her own life and highly injurious emotionally and physically to her, leading to all manner of physical troubles. She began to pray for her associates every morning and night, as follows: "All my co-workers are known in Divine Mind. God is guiding them. Divine love fills their minds and hearts. God's river of peace saturates their whole beings. God loves them and cares for them, and I radiate love, peace and goodwill to all of them."

I explained to her that when the angry, resentful

thoughts came to her mind, she was to immediately supplant them with spiritual thoughts, such as "God loves you and cares for you." This new attitude healed her of her self-righteousness, sense of condemnation and criticism. She completely recovered and discovered the value of praying for others, enabling her to get outside herself and drop all the negatives from her mind.

Tennyson said:

> For how are men better than sheep or goats
> If, knowing God, they lift not hands in prayer,
> For those they love and those who call them
>   friend,
> For so the whole round earth is every way
> Bound by gold chains about the feet of God.

Emperor Marcus Aurelius, the famous Roman philosopher and stoic, said: "Whatsoever any man doth or saith, thou must be good; not for any man's sake, but for thine own nature's sake; as if either gold or the emerald, or purple, should ever be saying to themselves, whatsoever any man doth or saith, I must still be an emerald, and I must keep my color."

Are You Tense When Visiting a High Personage?

When visiting one whom you consider to be a very prominent or any great personage, be sure to send your messengers before you to prepare the way. Affirm: "Divine love goes before me making straight, happy and joyous my way. I send the messengers of peace, harmony, joy, love and goodwill before me and they follow my orders implicitly. The Spirit in me salutes the Spirit in ________ and there are harmony, peace and Divine understanding between us. We are both blessed." Affirm these truths until you believe them in your heart. You will know when you believe them because your mind will be at peace.

The stoic philosopher Epictetus, who lived in the first century, said: "When you are going in to any great personage, remember that Another (God), also from above, sees what is going on, and that you ought to please Him rather than the other."

Never Seek Revenge or a Desire to Get Even

Listen to the ancient philosopher Epictetus: "Shall I not hurt him who has hurt me? Consider first what hurt means. For if good consists in my choice of action, and the evil also is my choice of action, see if what you say is not this: what then? Since that man has hurt himself by doing an unjust act to me, shall I not hurt myself by doing an unjust act to him?"

You Are Wonderful

Did you ever consider how wonderful you are and what tremendous potentialities lie at the unplumbed depths of your mind? All the powers and qualities of God reside in your subjective depths, waiting to be called upon and utilized. You are here to discover how capable, how great and how noble and Godlike you are. You are here to lead a full and happy life.

Cease believing the old way. Shed the old garments of sick man, poor man, deaf man. Get out of the old ruts; break away from your childhood pattern. Do you sing the same old hymns and visit the same old pew in the church? Do you still believe everything grandmother and grandfather told you about God, life and the universe? Are you still thinking the dead thoughts of dead men which today, in the light of science and knowledge, are completely false? Millions of people today have weird, grotesque, outlandish beliefs about God and the laws of life, which any high school boy knows is absolutely false and ridiculous. Let the truth and the sunshine of God's love enter your mind and heart, and become a new being.

They Said It Might Be Fatal

I had a very interesting conversation with a woman in Las Vegas. The surgeon and her personal physician said that her case seemed terminal and that she might die during the operation. She decided, nevertheless, to go ahead with the operation. She prayed for guidance, and also asked the "Secrets of the I Ching"* to comment on her operation for the next day. She received Hexagram 42, which seemed to confirm her own intuitive decision.

*See *Secrets of the I Ching* by Dr. Joseph Murphy, Parker Publishing Company, West Nyack, N.Y., 1970.

The night before the operation she invited to her home some of her Truth friends—students of the Science of Mind—and they sang songs and engaged in a festive evening—song, wine and food. Her attitude of mind banished all fear—the operation was successful. That was five years ago, and today she is very much alive and free from all pain. She is completely healed. She met the problem and overcame it. Her faith in the Miraculous Healing Power brought about the so-called miracle of healing.

Watch Your Words

The late Dr. Frederick Bailes, one of the great teachers in Los Angeles for many years, told me of a friend of his who used to say to him, "Bailes, all members of my family passed on when they reached seventy-two. I will be seventy-two next year, and that's it."

Dr. Bailes told his friend of the dangers of making such a statement, as his subconscious would accept it. He paid no attention, though, and on his seventy-second birthday he dropped dead in the street. He had decreed his own demise. The Bible says: *For by thy words thou shalt be justified, and by thy words thou shalt be condemned* (Matthew 12:37).

Others say, "I'm too old now. I won't last much longer. You know, I am sixty-five." These suggestions of weakness, decrepitude and old age enter into the subconscious mind and come forth after their kind. Let your words heal, bless and inspire yourself and everybody else.

She Said, "I'm Going to Die Here"

Recently I visited a woman in the local hospital, and she said to me, "I know I am going to die here. People are dying in this place every day."

I said to her, "You should change your attitude and affirm, 'I am alive with the Life of God. I am now at home with my husband, doing what I love to do.' "

Her doctor said that there was no reason why she could not get well and live for many years. I told her husband what she was saying, and he and the doctor agreed that she was well enough to go home. He brought her home and she is now rejoicing in being back in her own condominium.

Her husband broke the fear thoughts in her mind. Had she continued making those negative statements, she would undoubtedly have passed on in the hospital. The subconscious takes no jokes, and it is foolish and stupid to make such statements as she did.

You Should Teach Along These Lines

As I write this chapter, I have just received a wonderful Christmas letter from a woman in another state saying that I had told her at one of the International New Thought Congresses that she should teach along these lines. Probably this was an intuitive perception on my part at that time. She said that she had taken many courses, but was timid, shy and fearful of appearing before a group; yet, she had remarkable results as a counsellor.

She began to think about what I said—that Life flows from the inside to the outside, from thought to thing, from subjective to objective, and from Spirit to manifestation. She began to teach in her home, starting with five students, and is now a very successful minister along New Thought lines. Fear had held her back. She had been saying to herself, "Maybe in five years I will be ready," not realizing that in five years' time she would say the same thing. Her desire to teach and communicate the truth to others was the impulse of the Life-Principle in her seeking expression.

This Universal Life-Principle, called God, is in all of us and is forever seeking expression through us. She said in her letter that she welcomed the idea in her mind to teach. Encouragement came from others and all doors opened up to fulfill her dreams. The longings, the yearnings, the urges and inner aspirations of your heart are God-given. Welcome them; accept them and claim boldly: "God gave me this desire. It is good and very good. God opens up the way for its perfect manifestation." Begin now and prove it to yourself.

Be Ye Doers of the Word

If you want to become a great chemist, you must study and apply yourself diligently, learning all the principles of chemistry. As you grow in knowledge and awareness of the laws underlying chemistry, you will command prestige, recognition and advancement. If you wish to play music and become outstanding in your profession, you must study music. Fall in love with it; then you can play a melody of God for all of us. The great surgeon is in demand everywhere, but he had to study for many years anatomy and surgery and the various principles underlying his technique, in order to qualify and be successful.

There are the laws of mind which must be learned and practiced before we can have and do the things we desire to do. To be is to have. You must be the great musician: Study, and then recognition comes. You succeeded through application and devotion in understanding and conviction. The thrill is in the music. The joy comes in achievement of a job well done.

Your thought becomes things. It is not a question of mind over matter. Matter is simply the Spirit in you condensed into matter so that it is visible to your three-dimensional frame of reference. Your thought becomes the things—the book, the invention, the new device, the novel, the trip, etc. They are all in your mind as thought images. Your thought and feeling become matter. You don't make grapes out of thistles by thinking, as each seed grows after its kind. But if you were hungry for grapes and you really wanted them, then you would attract grapes by believing you have them now. Your expectancy and confidence would attract grapes to you.

Every Problem Has an Answer

You may have a desire to be, to do, or to have and you find a fear-thought enters in, challenging your desire or ideal. There is something in your mind that seems to oppose your objective or goal. To bring about a solution, you have to exalt the possibility of bringing your desire to pass and neutralize the negative thought. It is no use to deny that the negative thought is there. Reason things out from a spiritual standpoint.

Your fear is based on the fact that you think external circumstances and conditions are causative. Externals are an effect, not a cause. Realize this simple truth and the fear will be dissolved. Claim that God gave you the desire, and Infinite Spirit within you will reveal the perfect plan for its unfoldment. There is now no opposition in your mind. As you adhere to the fulfillment of your desires, it will come to pass.

Change the Mind and You Change the Body

A student asked me how she should pray about her physical condition. She was denying the arthritis with which she was afflicted, and the medicine she was taking provided little or no relief. I suggested that she cease denying, because to deny is to affirm. All she had to do was to change her mind and forget the inflammation in her body. She was not to say, "I don't have arthritis, pain," etc. These symptoms are not "unreal" but are manifestations of a disturbed, agitated mind based on suppressed rage and hostility.

Her job was to bless the doctor, knowing that he was Divinely guided in all ways, and right action reigned supreme. The pain she experienced was a warning that something needed to be corrected in her subconscious mind where the problem was. She had felt a deep-seated, unresolved resentment and was full of hostility toward another student. She now began to fill her subconscious with life-giving patterns, knowing that she would crowd out of her mind all the negative patterns submerged there.

She prayed as follows: "God is guiding my doctor. He is God's man, and whatever he does can only bless me. I forgive myself for harboring this sleeping grudge and hostility toward __________ and I wish for her all the blessings of life. I mean this. I am sincere, and it is finished and done. God's Healing Love is focussed at that point in my subconscious where the problem is, and it is shattered, making way for the Holy Spirit to flow through me. My soul (subconscious mind) is restored, and I give thanks. My mind is stayed on God and His Healing Power. *Thou wilt keep him in perfect peace, whose mind is stayed on thee* . . . (Isaiah 26:3)."

In due time she healed herself.

Getting a Sense of Oneness

After this manner, therefore, pray ye: Our Father which art in heaven . . . (Matthew 6:9). The word "which" indicates you are dealing with a universal, impersonal, Presence available to all people. It is available to the altruist and the agnostic, as well as to the holy man. This Presence is limitless, timeless, spaceless and ageless. You can make It personal by appropriating more of love, light, truth, beauty, peace and harmony. This Presence responds to all who call upon It.

"Our Father" indicates that all of us have a common Father. It is the One Life animating all things. It also means that we are all brothers and sisters and intimately related, because It is the same Life-Principle operating in all of us. We have a common Source and are made of the same universal substance.

Realize your sense of oneness with all people when you pray and wish for everyone all the blessings of life. It takes over four billion people in the world to tell you who you are. They are all extensions of yourself. To be angry or resentful toward others or animals or anything that God created destroys your sense of unity and oneness with the Divine Presence. All men and women, all animals, and everything else in the universe came from a common Source. It follows, therefore, that no one thing can be in opposition to another. Spirit (God) is one and indivisible, and all things are Spirit made manifest. Spirit can't fight

Itself. This is why it is written: . . . *All things work together for good to them that love God* . . . (Romans 8:28). That applies to all those who understand the nature of the Life-Principle. Establish in your mind the law of unity, and wonders will happen as you pray.

The Upanishads, a mystic teaching forming many portions of the early Vedas of India, are among the most astounding productions of the human mind in any age or country. The following are quotations from the Maitri Upanishad: "Let a man strive to purify his thoughts. What a man thinketh, that is he; this is the eternal mystery. Dwelling with God with thoughts serene, he will obtain imperishable happiness. If the thoughts of a man were so fixed on Brahma (God) as they are on the things of the senses, who would not then be free from bondage?"

CHAPTER 6

Taking Control

You can take control of your thoughts because you are the boss and your thoughts are your employees. You tell them where they are to direct their attention. You want your thoughts to pay dividends and increase your health and wealth. Your thoughts are the coin of your mental world. Change your thoughts and keep them changed. Your thoughts generate emotions and your thoughts and feelings control your destiny. If you do not take charge of your own thoughts, then the thoughts and moods of others will control you and order you around like a slave. Never permit your thoughts and emotions to run riot, as then you will have lost all control.

She Was a Nervous Wreck

A woman said to me, "I am constantly upset by my relatives. Nearly everything they say upsets me. I feel slighted and insulted. My mind has taken hold of the idea that they don't like me and resent me, and I can't get rid of it." All this was due to her morbid imagination. She saw slights and hurts where none were intended.

She decided to break the spasm, as it was caused by her habitual negative thinking. She began to affirm every time any one of them came to her mind, "God loves you. God be with you." She made a habit of this, and after some days she broke the spasm altogether, because she had established a new habit in her mind.

Normal Concern

When a loved one is ill or in the hospital, you have a normal concern for his or her well-being. You overcome anxiety by realizing that the healing power of God is flowing through your loved one and that God's love saturates the mind and heart of that person, knowing also that God is guiding all those who minister to your loved one. A normal concern is not anxiety or fear. You are concerned, but constructive in your attitude and not dejected and depressed. There are some men and women who are walking zombies. They use Valium, Librium and other sedatives, and they seem to have no concern for anything in particular.

How He Handles Neurotics

A doctor friend of mine here in Leisure World said to me that when a neurotic comes to him (and he defines a neurotic as one who thinks confusedly about many things which are not true), he suggests that the person become active in the hospital. There are many opportunities for such people to give of their time and ability. As they care for others and get interested, their own condition improves remarkably. The reason for this is that they are releasing love and goodwill.

He suggests to others that they get involved in music or gardening or some hobby which appeals to them. He said that as they get involved in these outer activities and give of their time and talent, they heal themselves. In some English hospitals they get the mentally disturbed patients to make toys for children, tool leather and make various trinkets and other useful objects. This activity takes the mental patient out of himself and results in healing of the mind.

The Inside Controls the Outside

Recently I talked with a man who was terribly concerned about his two young sons, his business, his home life and the security of his family, as he was away so much on business. I explained to him that the inside (his thought and feeling) controls external conditions and experiences. Thoughts are things, and the Spirit in him is God, the Only Presence, Power, Cause and Substance. Thoughts take form.

I gave him a special prayer to use three times out loud in the morning and also at night. I suggested that he memorize some paragraphs during the day, and when fear-thoughts came to him, to affirm at once, "God loves me and God loves and takes care of my home and family." I added that after a period of time, these Godlike thoughts would become a habit. The special prayer follows:

"God is all there is. One with God is a majority. *If God be for me who can be against me?* (Romans 8:31). I know and believe God is the Living Spirit Almighty—the Ever-Living One, the All-Wise One—and there is no power to challenge God. I know and accept completely that when my thoughts are God's thoughts, God's power is with my thoughts of good. I know I cannot receive what I cannot give, so I direct thoughts of love, peace, light and goodwill to this person or persons (mention name or names) and to everyone else. I am immunized and God-intoxicated, and I am always surrounded by the sacred circle of God's love. The whole armor of God surrounds me and enfolds me. I am Divinely guided and directed, and I enter into the joy of living. . . . *In thy presence is fulness of joy; at thy right hand there are pleasures for evermore* (Psalm 16:11)."

The practice of this prayer is creative meditation, and the regular application of it brought peace to his troubled mind. When troubled, focus your attention on all the thoughts which make for peace of mind.

Cause of Warfare in Mind

If you have an intense desire to do something and also a belief that you cannot do it, this is warfare and is also disease. A boy had acne all over his face. He had an intense desire to become an air pilot, but his father objected and made him work in his grocery store. The skin is the individuality of a person. Clean skin indicates clean blood. The father of the boy was made to understand the cause of the boy's acne and his frustration, so he permitted him to prepare for the career he desired. The skin condition disappeared. The skin is an envelope of God's love.

Watch Your Thoughts

A man I knew in England was afraid his money would be destroyed in a suitcase. He cautioned, or ordered, his wife (men order their wives in England) to let everything burn but the money in case of fire. Fire occurred some years later when both were away, and the suitcase and everything else were destroyed. Job said, . . . *The thing which I greatly feared is come upon me* . . . (Job 3:25). Let your words be words of wisdom, truth and beauty.

Some years ago I read that the captain of the Titanic always paced the deck wondering what he would do in case of disaster, and then disaster finally came. However, one man's consciousness could not sink a ship, provided others had the right thoughts, as there is a balance throughout all nature. Fear is contagious, but so are love, faith, confidence, enthusiasm and laughter. Fear kills. Shock kills due to chemical changes in the body. Fear of old age causes one to grow old, wrinkled and withered.

Recently an engineer seventy-five years of age applied for a position which was not open to men of his age. He assumed in his mind that the position was his: he was hired. Either the employer failed to see his age in the application or simply did not care. He had all the qualifications. You must be convinced first, not the employer.

How a General Solved His Problem

Many years ago, I read an interesting article about General Cynaresky who fought during the Napoleonic War. He and his staff were discussing strategy: how to combat successfully the French army. He listened for a few minutes and brushed aside all their suggestions regarding General Staff mapping strategy. He went off to sleep with the one consuming idea—victory—and he saw the end.

It is said that he snored while they conducted the discussion. He had his plan and did not want to be swayed. He went to sleep, repeating to himself over and over again, "Victory," and undoubtedly succeeded in impregnating his subconscious mind. His deeper mind responded and brought forth results in conformity with the impression in his subconscious. He was instrumental in defeating Napoleon.

Your subconscious mind is deductive. It takes all impressions given it as facts. It is wholly impersonal; it accepts the idea as existing *now* and acts accordingly.

How She Became a TV Singer

A young singer had received many rejections as she attempted to get a position to perform professionally. One night she fell into a sort of sleep, a drowsy state.

She felt completely relaxed. She could hear the clock tick and the baby cry, but she had no desire to move. This sleepy state brought about an outcropping of her subconscious mind, and her conscious mind was partially submerged.

In this passive state she said, "I want to be a singer on TV." She had already framed her request; then she condensed it down to one word, "TV." She then sank into a deep sleep, repeating the one word, "TV." A few days later she was accepted. She had succeeded in impressing her subconscious mind. She got into that passive, psychic, receptive state of mind of heightened suggestibility or increased susceptibility to suggestion, which is an easy, simple way of impregnating the subconscious mind.

The Psalmist says, *Thou hast put gladness in my heart. . . . I will both lay me down in peace, and sleep: for thou, Lord, only makest me dwell in safety* (Psalm 4:7–8).

When Will My Prayer Be Answered?

Seeds mature at different periods, according to their kind. Likewise, seeds, or impressions made in the subconscious mind, mature at different periods: days, weeks, months or years. *But of that day and that hour knoweth no man, no, not the angels which are in heaven, neither the Son, but the Father. . . . Ye know not when the master of the house cometh, at even, or at midnight, or at the cockcrowing . . .* (Mark 13:32–35).

The reason something turns up which you did not expect is this: Perhaps, for example, some years ago you were in business and your partner stole money. You think of it now, and you get very excited. You live the role over again. It is not withered, it is not forgotten, it is not forgiven. The root is there yet, but would not be there if you had completely forgiven. The proof of forgiveness is: If you can remember the episode and remain indifferent altogether and with no particular feeling about it, then you have forgiven. You live the scene over again, you create it in your mind, and like the seed that recedes and grows again quarterly, annually, biennually (for example, certain plants die and bud again according to season), your old condition appears in a new form and you wonder where it came from.

The proof that you are free of bitterness and antagonism is this: Are you able to see the other person as happy, harmonious, joyous and free? If not, you have not forgiven or forsaken. These are the weeds you must pluck out. The roots are there, and roots wither by Divine indifference. Kill the root by wishing for them all the blessings of life. Mean it, decree it, loose them and let them go. According to your decision is it done unto you.

Happy in Spite of

Some people say, "I'm happy in spite of," and not "because of." You must be happy *because of.*

If, for example, John Jones next door is out of a job and you say, "I'm better off than he is; I'm working. I am glad, I am happy and I will be happy in spite of the conditions around me," you are acknowledging lack, are you not? You are being stoical about it. You must be happy because you have decreed happiness, peace, harmony and abundance. When your mood or feeling is natural, you do not at the same time become conscious of lack all around you and dwell on it, because that mood of lack and limitation will be expressed by you.

He Did Not Really Love Her

A woman said to me that she was in love with a certain man, but that, unfortunately, he was not in love with her. She didn't seem to recognize that simple truth. I explained to her that if he really loved her he would take her everywhere and that he would not see her only in a shady hotel where no one he knew would see them. He never took her to meet his family or to meet his friends at his private club. When he saw a friend coming down the street, he would cause her to join him in running in to the nearest store, lest he be seen. He feels that he does not want to offer excuses for his actions. He has not accepted love as a real thing or a fact. If he had, he would take her everywhere.

She subsequently discovered that he was already married and had been lying to her for three years.

You should do everything openly, because you can't conceal anything indefinitely.

Joyous Expectancy

A man said to me that he could not experience a sensation about something he has not experienced. Suppose I told you the most wonderful thing happened, and yet did not tell you what it was, but held you in suspense for several minutes, building up the wonderful thing. Could you not experience joy and expectancy? Of course, you could. You can enter into a feeling regarding the happy ending of a protracted law suit.

Praying is the same thing. You pray for something you have not yet experienced, but you accept the reality of the idea or thought-image in your mind, knowing that an Almighty Power will bring it to pass.

Blind Faith Gets Results

Recently I had an interesting talk with a man who had returned from Israel. He said his father had been suffering from what is called terminal cancer. This young man constructed a story about how he had obtained a piece of the true cross from a monk in one of the monasteries in Israel, for which he paid five hundred dollars. His father, who is a devout Catholic, believed his son and was overjoyed. He placed the object on his abdominal area overnight, and to the amazement of his doctor, X-rays showed that the affliction had disappeared.

The subconscious had responded to his blind belief. The cross was a piece of wood the son had picked up from a tree. His father believed and was healed. You might call it an instantaneous cure by his father's blind belief in the magic power of the touch of the true cross.

Do not try to shake people's belief or give them a new philosophy of life when they are not ready to receive it. It's their crutch, and if you take away their crutch they fall.

Perpetual Motion

Many men talk of perpetual motion. The only perpetual motion, though, is your own consciousness, or Awareness, I AMness. It is Self-Existence and is eternal and requires no other power. It is the initial velocity or vibration; therefore, all other vibrations are lesser vibrations of the one. For example, if you fix something definitely in your consciousness, it is arrested in this motion; that is, it is completely accepted in your mind. It must be objectified.

Your Religion

Your religion is your relationship with God. If it makes you happy, contented, and you get comfort from it, don't try and force your opinion on others.

Recently a Lutheran girl was very ill and a Unity minister said to her, "Put your hand in mine and we will pray together to Jesus." This girl became healed. She believed in a personal Jesus to heal; and according to her belief was it done unto her.

If half the people really believed in their religions this would be a vastly different world. If a person is ill, don't say to him, "You had the wrong thoughts," or, "Your religious belief is all wrong." In that way you only make him worse. When he is healed you can, if he is agreeable, explain the laws of mind to him. Don't take a man's creed or belief away from him unless you give him something better instead—something that he can use and thereby become a greater, nobler, and more dignified character. There is truth behind the many rituals, ceremonies, rules and formulations. The truth seems to be covered all over with a thick cloud, and you must find the hidden meaning behind the symbols and rituals.

A Longing to Believe

A longing to believe is not real belief. To believe is to accept something as true, to live in the state of being it, to be alive to the truth. A woman in a local hospital who had a malignant tumor read some pamphlets published by Unity School, a wonderful teaching organization, and refused an operation. Her friend said, "This teaching is bad." The woman read the words about remarkable healings in the pamphlet and said to her, "This is what I've been waiting for."

This type of thinking is like the seed that was dropped on stony ground and flourished but then withered away—a passing mood or fancy which sounded good. She similarly tried the prayers, but they didn't work because she had no conviction.

. . . *Faith is the substance of things hoped for, the evidence of things not seen.* (Hebrews 11:1). Substance means confidence. Her minister explained to her that if she had the necessary faith in the healing power of God, she would not be in the hospital in the first place, and he suggested that she cooperate with her surgeon, as all healing is spiritual. She agreed, with excellent results. Remember, a longing for faith is not true faith. According to your faith is it done unto you.

You Can't Buy Respect or Dignity

Many think they can buy respect and dignity. They cannot. For example, the late Benito Mussolini of Italy knew he did not have the dignity of Haile Selassie. Selassie was a king and said at that time, "I will return to my land as a king and a conqueror." History reveals that Mussolini eventually lost prestige and met an untimely end. He would love to have had the honor, but he did not feel it and could not claim it in consciousness. Hitler strutted before his generals; he seized power, demanding prestige and honor. But he was always conscious of his deep inferiority complex.

Likewise, there are those who believe they can buy

their way into a select club; that they can buy respect. They cannot. The bell boy and other attendants of the club give more respect to the man who can barely pay his dues, because he has the consciousness of being a dignified person and demands respect. The queen is not conscious of doing wrong; therefore, no one accuses her of doing wrong, even though she may violate certain codes established by the public. She is still a queen and has no consciousness of guilt.

Many people of various religious beliefs feel guilty if they eat meat, drink wine, dance, wear gold or drink coffee; and when they violate these weird "don'ts" they feel guilty and suffer accordingly. Paul says: . . . *There is nothing unclean of itself: but to him that esteemeth any thing to be unclean, to him it is unclean* (Romans 14:14).

Success Is a Mental Attitude

A shoemaker wanted to open a shop in a certain street where there were not very many stores. It was practically deserted. Friends said to him that he should open up a place next to a big shoe repair shop elsewhere and he would benefit from their expensive advertising. He did that and was successful. Another man, however, opened up a shop in the deserted spot that the former had turned down and was also very successful, illustrating that evidence of senses is of no avail and is fallacious.

You propound a theory or proposition and another

will give you an equally good argument against it. There are two sides to every proposition. Within you is all knowledge, all power; the Infinite cannot fail. God is always successful in all His undertakings, whether making a new cosmos or a new star. God indwells you. Remember, you were born to win, to succeed and to triumph in life.

Banish Anxiety

The Lord is my light and my salvation; whom shall I fear? The Lord is the strength of my life; of whom shall I be afraid? This one verse of the Twenty-seventh Psalm gives personal freedom from all fear. It reveals to you the source of all power, strength, and wisdom. It enables you to reject the power of externals, takes the burden off your shoulders, and sets you on the high road to peace of mind, health, and happiness.

The Lord is the Presence of God, the I AM within you. In simple, psychological language, the Lord is your consciousness. What is consciousness? Your state of consciousness is the way you think, feel, believe, and the reasoning behind your belief. The cause of all your experiences is your thought and feeling.

Refuse to give power to conditions, circumstances, and the external world. Your thought initiates causation. Your thinking is cause; the condition is not causative. There is no power to challenge Omnipotence; therefore, there is nothing to fear. If fear comes to your mind, go within to your Divine Center; think of God and His Power, realizing that there is only One Power, and that you are one with It now. In this stillness, nothing external can inhibit, obstruct, or thwart you. Think of new and better conditions, the way you want things to be. Realize that as you think, it is Omnipotence thinking and moving on your behalf. The outcome is sure and certain, for it is God in action.

God is the name for the One Power acting beneficently in your life. This Power is Sovereign, Supreme, One and Indivisible. It is Self-moving. This Power inspires you, guides you, watches over you, strengthens you, and protects you in ways you know not of. God lives and reigns in your life. A realization of this truth is your salvation.

CHAPTER 7

The Royal Road to Victory

The wilderness and the solitary place shall be glad for them; and the desert shall rejoice, and blossom as the rose.

It shall blossom abundantly, and rejoice even with joy and singing: the glory of Lebanon shall be given unto it, the excellency of Carmel and Sharon, they shall see the glory of the Lord, and the excellency of our God.

Strengthen ye the weak hands, and confirm the feeble knees.

Say to them that are of a fearful heart, Be strong, fear not: behold, your God will come with vengeance, even God with a recompence; he will come and save you.

Then the eyes of the blind shall be opened, and the ears of the deaf shall be unstopped.

Then shall the lame man leap as an hart, and the tongue of the dumb sing: for in the wilderness shall waters break out, and streams in the desert.

> *And the parched ground shall become a pool, and the thirsty land springs of water: in the habitation of dragons, where each lay, shall be grass with reeds and rushes.*
>
> *And an highway shall be there, and a way, and it shall be called The way of holiness; the unclean shall not pass over it; but it shall be for those: the wayfaring men, though fools, shall not err therein.*
>
> *No lion shall be there, nor any ravenous beast shall go up thereon, it shall not be found there; but the redeemed shall walk there:*
>
> *And the ransomed of the Lord shall return, and come to Zion with songs and everlasting joy upon their heads: they shall obtain joy and gladness, and sorrow and sighing shall flee away.* (Isaiah 35:1–10)

The Book of Isaiah teaches that deliverance from problems, receiving abundant supply, wholeness and right action, as well as all other forms of good, come to man through God, which is your Higher Self or the I AM within you. The word Isaiah means God is salvation, spiritual understanding and awareness. As you recognize the Almighty Power within you and call upon It, you will discover a mighty vortex into which this Divine Presence pours Its light, love, truth and beauty to enrich your life.

The 35th Chapter of Isaiah is considered one of the

great spiritual masterpieces and is also one of the most beautiful, soul-stirring prayers in the Bible. Prayer changes the person who prays, and prayer is the contemplation of the truths of God from the highest standpoint. In prayer you do not try to change God; you discover all you can about the eternal verities, the laws of life and the principles of love, peace, beauty, joy, abundance, truth, harmony, etc. Then claim that what is true of God is true of you.

In prayer you fill your subconscious mind with the great eternal truths, which are the same yesterday, today and forever. As you fill your deeper mind with these great truths, you crowd out of your mind everything unlike God or the Truth. It is your subconscious beliefs, convictions and assumptions which take executive control of your life. That is why Phineas Parkhurst Quimby said in 1847, "Man is belief expressed."

There Is Always an Answer

During the recent Christmas season I counselled a young girl who was finishing her third year in college but could not return because her father had lost his executive position and could not afford the large fee for the university for a fourth year. She followed a simple prayer, affirming frequently: "God opens up the way for me to finish my fourth year at the university in Divine law and order." She practiced this affirmation, realizing that she was inscribing this request by repetition, faith and expectancy in her subconscious mind.

After several days she became quiet in her mind and was at peace about it. On Christmas Eve, her grandmother, who had never before given her any kind of a gift, suddenly presented her with a check for $3,000, adding that she should let her know whenever she needed further financial help in college. The answer came in a way that she did not expect. She believed, however, and her subconscious responded accordingly.

Scientific prayer means that you recollect the truth about God, which brings about a change in your mentality. As a result of your change of mind, the outer condition changes, too. Remember, it is the change in feeling and conviction that gets results.

Verse 1: *The wilderness and the solitary place shall be glad for them; and the desert shall rejoice, and blossom as the rose.* Remember that the Bible is full of Oriental symbols and similes. The writers of the Bible were inspired and illumined from On High, and they wrote in the language of the era, using symbols, allegories, similes and the idiomatic expressions in use then.

We must, therefore, see the inner meaning. The desert spoken of could apply to all of us, because in the minds of millions of people there is nothing growing in their minds but the weeds of fear, ignorance, superstition, and weird and grotesque concepts of

God, Life and the Universe. All of us have been placed here to bring forth the fruits of wisdom, truth and beauty; furthermore, it is God's purpose for us to lead a full and happy life, expressing ourselves at the highest level and exercising our faculties at the highest degree. The greatest desert in the world is not in the Sahara or in Arizona, but under the hat of man.

Literally speaking, the French have done marvelous things in the Sahara, locating riches in the ground, establishing cities, schools and industries, and discovering oil and many other mineral resources. The same applies to other parts of the world, such as Israel, which turned a vast wilderness and desert into a beehive of productive activity. It was the existence of the Infinite Intelligence in men that enabled them to discover the riches of the soil under their feet. The riches had been there for thousands of years—yes, for millions of years—but man discovered the riches of his mind, which in turn enabled him to find the riches of the soil. The real wealth was in the mind of man.

His Desert Rejoiced and Blossomed as the Rose

Recently a great number of fires burned down some beautiful homes, some undoubtedly set by arsonists. A professor told me that he had been away and, on his return, found his house burned to the ground. He said there was only one thing to do, and that was to turn to the Infinite Presence and Power within. He claimed out loud many times a day: "I am surrounded by Divine love and Divine peace, and God opens up a new door and a new way for me now. It is God in action."

He said that an opportunity suddenly came out of the blue, revealing the offer of a wonderful promotion and in another university, which provided him with new quarters, greater prestige, more money and greater recognition. The solitary place and the wilderness he witnessed became glad, and his insurance will compensate him for some of his losses.

Look for the chink of light where the problem is. When the problem is most acute and darkness is all around you, the Light comes. Epictetus said, "What else can I do, a lame old man, but sing hymns to God?"

Verse 2: *It shall blossom abundantly, and rejoice even with joy and singing: the glory of Lebanon shall be given unto it, the excellency of Carmel and Sharon, they shall see the glory of the Lord, and the excellency of our God.*

Here you are informed that when you give attention to the riches of the Infinite, which are everywhere, your subconscious mind always magnifies and multiplies exceedingly whatever you deposit in it. Nature is lavish, extravagant, bountiful and even wasteful. Look at all the fruit that rots in the tropics, for example, probably enough to feed all of humanity. The desert will blossom and grow anything when you water it.

Lebanon is a range of mountains in Northern Palestine and is noted for its cedars, also for the grandeur and beauty of the surrounding area. Lebanon means lovely, noble, God-like thoughts. Carmel is a range of hills in Palestine, whose soil is very rich. Spiritually speaking, it means that you realize the tremendous possibilities under the Divine Law, which means that we become what we contemplate. Your mind is a garden, and as you meditate and contemplate the riches of the Infinite, spiritual, mental, intellectual, financial and social, you will be impelled, propelled and compelled to express the riches of God in all phases of your life.

Sharon means fruitful, prosperous. In other words, the fruits of the Spirit are love, joy, peace, gentleness, beauty, harmony, goodness, faith, receptivity and a balanced mind. True religion brings forth these fruits. That is why it is written, *Ye shall know them by their fruits. . . .* (Matthew 7:16). The writer of this part of the Bible engages in a magnificent poetic rhapsody as he elaborates on the wonders and glories that come to you when you contemplate the wonders of the One, the Beautiful and the Good. He says you shall see the glory of the Lord. Glory means glow or love, and ray means light. In other words, you shall experience the love, the light and the goodness of God in all your undertakings.

Plato, speaking of love, said: "Yes, Love, who showers benignity upon the world, and before whose presence all harsh passions flee and perish; the author of all soft affections; the destroyer of all ungentle thoughts; merciful, mild, the object of the admiration of the wise, and the delight of the gods; possessed by the fortunate, and desired by the unhappy, therefore unhappy because they possess him not."

The Secret Place

And he said unto them, Come ye yourselves apart into a desert place, and rest a while: for there were many coming and going, and they had no leisure so much as to eat (Mark 6:31).

In a different sense, the desert symbolizes the secret place in your own mind where you communicate with your Higher Self or the I AM within you. It is where you turn away from the evidence of senses and the objective world and contemplate the Divinity within you which shapes your ends. It is where you put God first in your life, which is that formless Spirit from which all things flow. You are in the Secret Place of the Most High when you turn to God within you in prayer and reverence.

Here in this communion with the Divine, you are free from distractions of the outside world and you feed on the spiritual bread of heaven, which is harmony, peace, inspiration, guidance and Divine right action. As you do this, you will find your mind is at peace and the desert of your mind will rejoice and blossom as the rose.

Verses 3 and 4: *Strengthen ye the weak hands, and confirm the feeble knees. Say to them that are of a fearful heart, Be strong, fear not: behold, your God will come with vengeance, even God with a recompence; he will come and save you.*

The Lord in the Bible means the power of the Almighty operating in you, through you and all around you. With your hand you fashion, mold, create and shape. A policeman directs traffic with his hand; likewise, you can direct the power in a constructive and joyous way.

She Lifted the Truck

Recently I read about a frail woman who lifted a corner of a truck when her husband became caught underneath the wheel. Four men later could not even lift the heavy vehicle. She said, "I did not do it. I called on God and He gave me the strength." All the power of God is within. Call on It frequently and you will receive a response. You don't have to wait for emergencies in order to display or experience this power.

Recently a doctor friend of mine told me that he had been treating a man for several months who had been suffering from rheumatoid arthritis. His knees were somewhat crippled and partially immobilized. He had to use crutches every day while he worked in his store. A gangster came in one morning, though, and told him to open the safe. He said that he could not bend down and open it and that his wife had always opened the safe. The gunman said, "I'll give you thirty seconds to open the safe or I will blow your head off."

He opened the safe and the doctor said his knees are now supple, he can bend them, the calcareous deposits are diminishing, and the edema and pain have improved considerably. He is making wonderful progress and is no longer using crutches. In the annals of medicine it is well known that during great fright, emergencies, shock and tragedies, people do extraordinary things. Cripples walk and paralyzed people are suddenly healed. In the case of the man with crutches, the idea to save his life at all costs seized his mind, and the power of the Almighty responded. That is called touching the hem of His garment. The power was always there, but he had failed to use It.

How often have you heard the expression, "He is my right-hand man," meaning he is very competent, an excellent co-worker and a great adjunct to the particular person? When you were a guest of honor at some function, you probably noticed that you were placed at the right hand of the host, a symbol of respect, prestige and recognition for some outstanding work or achievement. As you know from your Latin in school, the word *manus* means mind, and the word *man* is a generic term in all Bibles, meaning the thinker. This applies to all men and women; it does not refer to man as a male. All of us are placed in our environments to dramatize, portray and manifest more of our Divinity here on earth.

Her Knees Were Shaking

A schoolteacher told me that during one of her examinations for a higher degree, her knees were actually shaking. Then she took hold of herself and began to affirm slowly and quietly the words from the 27th Psalm: *The Lord is my light and my salvation; whom shall I fear? the Lord is the strength of my life; of whom shall I be afraid?* (Psalm 27:1). Gradually her mind became quiet and relaxed, and as she quieted and stilled her mind, the answers came forth from her subconscious mind and she overcame her problem.

At an examination there are always a few easy questions. Answer these first; then, when your mind is relaxed and passive, the answers to the other questions will well up from your deeper mind. The greatest antidote to fear is the 27th Psalm.* Your acceptance and re-affirmation of the great truths embodied in the 27th Psalm will give you peace of mind and a spiritual healing.

. . . *God will come with vengeance, even God with a recompence; he will come and save you* (Isaiah 35:4). Vengeance in the Bible is a vindication of the

*See *Songs of God* by Joseph Murphy, DeVorss and Co., Inc., Marina del Rey, Ca., 1979.

Truth, which means you have received an answer to your prayer, proving the Truth which you affirmed, and you found peace in this changing world. The God-Presence never seeks revenge. All of us are thinkers and we are responsible for the way in which we think. If we begin to think negatively or destructively, we reap the results of our habitual thinking. This is why you are an individual. You are capable of choice. When you really learn to choose, you will choose from the Kingdom of God within you. The recompense spoken of means that retribution and reward come to you based on your habitual thinking, beliefs and action.

Verses 5 and 6: *Then the eyes of the blind shall be opened, and the ears of the deaf shall be unstopped. Then shall the lame man leap as an hart, and the tongue of the dumb sing: for in the wilderness shall waters break out, and streams in the desert.*

In these two verses you can easily perceive how the Biblical mystic soared to the heights in an exultant paean of praise regarding the miraculous healing power of God through prayer, meditation and mystic visioning. Millions are unfortunately spiritually blind to the powers of God within them. They do not know that thoughts are things, what we feel we attract, and what we imagine we become. Millions are blind to the laws of mind, for they do not know and realize that whatever they really believe (good or bad) will be expressed on the screen of space. These verses are saying that all things are possible with God.

She Was Blind

There is the well-known, duly authenticated case of Madame Bire. She was blind. Her optic nerves were atrophied, useless. She visited Lourdes and experienced what she termed a miraculous healing. Ruth Cranston, a Protestant investigator, wrote about healings at Lourdes in *McCall's* magazine, issue of November 1955. She said that at Lourdes Madame Bire had regained her sight, incredibly with the optic nerves still lifeless and useless, as several doctors could testify after repeated examinations. A month later, upon re-examination, it was found that the seeing mechanism had been restored to normal.

She was not healed by the waters of the shrine but by her blind belief or faith. She went to the shrine with expectancy and faith, knowing in her heart that she would receive a healing. Healings take place at various shrines around the world, at Shinto shrines, Buddhistic shrines and other so-called holy places.

There is only One Healing Presence which responds to each person according to his belief. *The ears of the deaf shall be unstopped.* Our ears must be open to the laws of life and the way of the Holy Spirit. *And in them is fulfilled the prophecy of Esaias, which saith, By hearing ye shall hear, and shall not under-*

stand; and seeing ye shall see, and shall not perceive: For this people's heart is waxed gross, and their ears are dull of hearing, and their eyes they have closed; lest at any time they should see with their eyes, and hear with their ears, and should understand with their heart, and should be converted, and I should heal them (Matthew 13:14–15).

There are millions of people who refuse to hear the Truth. They are steeped in the old traditional beliefs. They do not realize, and many refuse to accept, the fact that each person is his own savior; that he molds, fashions and creates his own destiny. Healing follows upon a change of the mind. When you change your mind, you change your body and your entire world. But the eyes (meaning spiritual perception) must see the truths of life, and the ears must be open and receptive to the good news. Ears represent hearing or understanding, and the heart must be open to the influx of Divine love. When people open their minds and hearts to the Infinite Healing Presence, a healing follows.

In the medical field today, marvelous results are achieved along all lines. Wholistic medicine is being practiced and taught in various cities throughout the country. Doctors are treating people from a spiritual, mental and physical standpoint, realizing that nothing happens in the body unless there is a corresponding mental cause in the subconscious mind. Cripples learn to walk and run, and the dumb speak also. We must remember that there are mental cripples. We also have moral cripples, unfortunately, which our newspapers attest to almost every day. When the Light of God's Truth penetrates their mind they learn to walk in the Light and are healed.

There are millions who can speak, sing and laugh, but the tongue also stands for the creative word of God. It is your faculty to speak the word of Truth which heals, blesses and inspires people. You can also speak in a new tongue when you think, speak and act from the Divine Center within you. The thief who robbed, cheated and defrauded people and is now an honest, upright man speaks in the tongue of honesty, integrity and justice. The Bible refers to the spiritually dumb who talk and speak about hell, damnation, sickness, gloom and doom, etc.

When verse 6 says, . . . *In the wilderness shall waters break out, and streams in the desert,* waters refers to Divine inspiration. A stream of creative ideas oftentimes comes to you when you pray and ask that you be inspired from On High. Then you are refreshed and rejuvenated.

They Were Dying of Thirst

Some years ago, I read a story about a sailing ship becalmed in Southern waters. They had no fresh water on board. It was extremely hot and there was no wind or soft breezes. Mouths and tongues were swollen, and the sailors' thirst was for water, as it meant the difference between life and death. A cup of water to them was worth more than its weight in gold. The captain espied a ship and he signalled her: "We have no fresh water; please give us water." The second ship signalled back, "Let down your buckets; you are in the mouth of the Amazon." The Amazon is the mighty river of South America, which sends its fresh waters 150 miles or more into the Atlantic Ocean. Fresh water was all around them.

Don't perish of thirst. Realize that the waters of life are waiting for you to let down your buckets and take all you want. It is foolish to pray for air; take all you want—there is no shortage. Tremendous potentialities are awaiting you. All you have to do is open your mind to receive. Shakespeare said: "All things be ready, if the mind be so." Ready your mind to receive the gifts of God proffered to you from the foundations of time.

Verse 7: . . . *In the habitation of dragons, where each lay, shall be grass with reeds and rushes.* Dragons represent hidden complexes in the recesses of your subconscious mind. These could refer to suppressed fears, hates and hostilities that we may have swept under the rug. Whatever is hidden in the subconscious must come forth sooner or later. The mystic writer promises that all these dragons can be eradicated and expunged from your subconscious mind through prayer, and your deeper mind will become a garden of God where grass, reeds and rushes grow, meaning a quiet and peaceful mind.

She Heard the Voice Say, "Kill Him!"

A woman told me that for several nights she had heard a voice saying to her, "Kill your father-in-law." This was her subconscious talking back to her. She had impressed hatred and hostility in her subconscious mind every night prior to sleep, and, while asleep, her subconscious responded accordingly. This was the dragon she created herself.

At my suggestion, she asked her father-in-law to leave her home and establish his own domicile, which he did. Out of sight, out of mind. She found it easy to release him to God, as follows: "I surrender __________ to God and I wish for him all the blessings of life. God's love fills my soul." She followed this spiritual prescription and succeeded in dissolving the complex. She knows now that God speaks in peace, harmony and love.

Verse 8: *And an highway shall be there, and a way, and it shall be called The way of holiness; the unclean shall not pass over it; but it shall be for those: the wayfaring men, though fools, shall not err therein.*

This is a very beautiful promise, and a promise in the Bible is a law. For tender beauty and splendor, it stands unique. The way of holiness is the way of wholeness, beauty and perfection. As you claim frequently, "I am a son (or daughter) of the Living God, and I am now expressing more and more of God's beauty, love, harmony and peace every moment of the day; the way of wholeness, beauty and perfection is being perfectly expressed through me now," you are making a triumphant and glorious mental journey back to God.

This is your manifesto and the way to escape from frustration, sickness and all limitation. Insist on peace, harmony, health and abundance. It is your right to lead a full and happy life, and it is your right and prerogative to see the Presence of God in others. Lift them in your thought, knowing that they are sons and daughters of God and heir to all of God's riches.

The trouble with millions of people is that they are downright lazy and indolent. All the powers of God are within them and they rarely, if ever, contact and utilize these powers. All of us know we are free to travel the highway. Murderers, thieves and holy men can travel the same highway. This is to remind you that God is no respecter of persons. The law is impersonal, and that applies to all laws. The highway is open to all; so is God open and receptive to all who call upon Him. God will answer the prayer of the atheist who says there is no God.

In other words, God answers every person's prayer according to that person's faith and belief in the heart. No one can block your contact with God. You don't need any ritual, ceremony or rite. You don't have to belong to any organization or believe in some creed. As you turn to this Divine Presence, It will respond to you. There are no barriers to your journey on the public highway. It is accessible to all. A "way" is the path in your own mind where you turn within yourself and contemplate the Presence of God within you, the Reality of you.

The Living Spirit Almighty is your Higher Self. You can commune with this Presence in the silence of your soul. This is where you walk and talk with God. You need no mediators, wine or wafers—only your own thought. Your thought mediates between the Invisible and the visible, and as you continue to contemplate the eternal verities, you will experience holiness which, as previously explained, means perfect health, harmony, peace and the life more abundant.

The "unclean" spoken of represent all those who have unclean thoughts, such as fear, hate, jealousy, doubt, sickness and ill will. These negative thoughts prevent them from experiencing harmony, health, peace and abundance. When you fill your mind with God-like thoughts and constructive imagery, the negative thoughts are destroyed and have no more power to hinder you on your journey back to God.

. . . The wayfaring men, though fools, shall not err therein. No matter how foolish you have been or how many mistakes you may have made, no matter how guilty you may feel, you can turn to the Divine

Presence this moment and claim: "Divine love fills my soul, Divine right action is mine now, and God's river of peace saturates my mind and heart." Forgive yourself for harboring negative thoughts and resolve to keep your mind clean from now on. God is Timeless and Spaceless. He never punishes. Change your mind now and keep it changed, and you will be on the path to holiness or wholeness in all phases of your life.

Verses 9 and 10: *No lion shall be there, nor any ravenous beast shall go up thereon, it shall not be found there; but the redeemed shall walk there: And the ransomed of the Lord shall return, and come to Zion with songs and everlasting joy upon their heads: they shall obtain joy and gladness, and sorrow and sighing shall flee away.*

It is recorded in the Bible that Daniel, when in the lion's den, turned his back on the lions and turned to the God-Presence within him. . . . *Thy God whom thou servest continually, he will deliver thee* (Daniel 6:16). Lions in the Bible represent seemingly very difficult situations of a threatening nature. Lions could also represent hidden complexes, a severe or so-called incurable sickness, or mountainous debt. Within every problem is the solution in the form of a desire. Therefore, turn your back upon the problem and focus your attention on the solution, knowing that the power and wisdom of God will reveal the solution. Continue in that belief and the problem will be dissolved in the light of God and His love.

The beasts mean any destructive or negative emotion that may well up within you; but now you know the solution and that is to let the sunshine of God's love enter into your subconscious mind. This is a very simple procedure. You can sit down now and affirm boldly for twenty minutes or half an hour: "God's love fills my soul." You will get a response and be healed. The beasts of fear, jealousy, envy and anger are completely neutralized and obliterated when you open your mind and heart to the influx of Divine love.

The "ransomed of the Lord" are all those men and women who have felt their oneness with the Infinite, which is their Higher Self, and constantly release light, love, truth and beauty. And they "shall return and come to Zion." Zion is an awareness of the Presence and Power of God within you. When you turn to this God-Presence, affirm freely, joyously and lovingly: "The joy, the wisdom and the peace of God reign supreme in my mind now." When you discover and realize that all the powers of the Godhead are within you and are responsive to your call, you will follow the injunction of the Psalmist:

> *Make a joyful noise unto the Lord, all ye lands.*

Serve the Lord with gladness: come before his presence with singing.

Know ye that the Lord he is God: it is he that hath made us, and not we ourselves; we are his people, and the sheep of his pasture.

Enter into his gates with thanksgiving, and into his courts with praise: be thankful unto him, and bless his name.

For the Lord is good; his mercy is everlasting; and his truth endureth to all generations. (Psalm 100)

Chapter 35 of Isaiah closes with six of the most beautiful words in all the Bible, giving you the absolute assurance that . . . *sorrow and sighing shall flee away.*

CHAPTER 8

Developing the Principles of Infinite Intelligence

It may be taken as an established fact that in proportion to the degree of advancement of knowledge of the Infinite Intelligence within man, the individual ceases to be subject to a mere law of averages (the mass mind—the race mind of four and a half billion people) and has a continually increasing power of controlling the condition of his own survival. When he learns of the Presence of God within him, man begins to choose wholeness, beauty and perfection. The down-and-out man is simply one who has forgotten the Divine Presence within himself.

The Bible says: . . . *The foxes have holes, and the birds of the air have nests; but the Son of man hath not where to lay his head* (Matthew 8:20). Truth is not usually popular and does not find ready lodgment in human minds and hearts. The average man does not listen when you tell him that he is his own savior, that he molds and fashions his own destiny and that he is responsible for his choices in this world.

You must be like the professional gambler and learn to "place all your chips on one sure thing," Which is the God-Presence within you, realizing that when you call the Infinite Presence and Power, It responds according to the nature of your request. Indulge in no idolatry of the past, such as the "good old days." This is childish, morbid self-pity and awakening nostalgia, preventing you from successfully pursuing the prize of harmony, health and peace.

Are Preachers and Teachers Unnecessary?

One way of answering this question is to accept the fact that we have had the Ten Commandments for thousands of years, which, if followed to the hilt by people of all walks of life, would make unnecessary the existence of any preachers and teachers. But in the clash of circumstances, the masses do not understand how to put into practice the laws implied in the terse words of the Ten Commandments, the Lord's Prayer, the Sermon on the Mount, the Pauline Epistles and the Four Gospels.

There are certain techniques and processes of prayer which must be followed before the potency of the Truth is sensed and felt by the individual. You don't violate the Sabbath by dancing or fishing on Sunday morning or by taking a hammer and some nails to work on the addition of a new room to the house. The esoteric violation of the Sabbath involves more than this. It actually has to do with a process in your mind which should lead to a true understanding of the Sabbath, which, in reality, means a sense of faith and abiding trust and conviction in the ever-availability of the Divine Presence here and now, in any emergency and without undue anxiety and pressure.

The Sabbath is the inner sense of peace and certitude which follows the impregnation of your subconscious mind. This is called the sixth day, or the length of time it took you to envelope your idea or desire with love and enthusiasm so that it was etched in your deeper mind. When this happens, there is an inner rest in which you no longer desire that for which you prayed. The interval of time between the impregnation of your subconscious and the manifestation on the objective plane is called the Sabbath.

There is a need for proper instruction in the ways and means whereby we can practice the Presence of God. When you really learn the Truth, you can begin to practice the eternal verities, which are the same yesterday, today and forever.

A Bastard Shall Not Enter Into the Congregation of the Lord . . . (Deuteronomy 23:2)

Many people are confused and troubled by this statement in the Bible, and they have a deep sense of guilt when a child is born out of wedlock. You must understand the inner meaning of the Bible; otherwise, you have nothing at all but the surface meaning. A false belief born out of real wedlock is but a son of a harlot (undisciplined emotion), which is ready to bring forth a bastard (negative condition) by uniting with any vagabond ideas such as hate, jealousy, fear or vengeance, which come along (your paramour). The children, or expressions of these emotions, bring on all manner of disease, and people do not know the cause or parents of the condition, which were actually their thoughts and emotions. A bastard does not know his own father; likewise, a man who does not know that his father is God, is considered in Biblical language to be an illegitimate child.

The woman at the well had five husbands* governed by the avalanches of sight, sound and sundry concepts of good and bad. In other words, her five senses were undisciplined and she was impregnating herself with all manner of false beliefs. . . . *Thy Maker is thine husband* . . . (Isaiah 54:5). In other words, God and His Truths should govern your conscious mind. That is the real husband. All negative thoughts and emotions are illegitimate, since they do not conform to the truths of God.

Who Answers Prayer?

You answer your own prayer, because whatever you really believe, your subconscious will bring to pass. You are told to pray believing, and you shall receive. The secret power in prayer is the art of be-

*See *John 4:16–18*

lieving that you have it already in your own mind, because the reality of everything is a thought-image in your mind. For example, if you have an invention which nobody knows about, is it not a reality in your mind? It has form, shape and substance in another dimension of mind and can be seen by a good psychic, clairvoyant or medium. It is real; you possess it now in your mind. As you accept it completely, you know that Infinite Intelligence Which gave you the idea will reveal the perfect plan for its unfoldment. The reality of everything is first a thought-image in the mind.

The Lord Shall Fight For You, and Ye Shall Hold Your Peace (Exodus 14:14)

Exodus 14:11 says: . . . *Because there were no graves in Egypt, hast thou taken us away to die in the wilderness?* . . . It is necessary to see the spiritual meaning of these words in order to perceive their profound significance.

Egypt means darkness, misery and limitation. Whatever we really believe in our heart (subconscious mind) can't be put out of sight. There is no possibility of bringing our hostility, anger or resentment into graves. Living in Egypt means living in bondage.

Pharaoh means your false beliefs and being governed by the five senses. Remember, your subconscious assumptions, emotional espousals and hidden conditioning rule and govern you.

Moses means to draw out; i.e., your desire for a

better life drives you into the wilderness—a place where you begin to think of the Presence and Power of God within you Which will bring you out of bondage into the Promised Land of harmony, health, peace and abundance.

Millions of people all over the world have wallowed "in Egypt" for centuries, exchanging one disease for another. In India it has been the bubonic plague, in the Middle Ages in Europe it was the black death, and in this century there is frequent reference to the white death—the degenerative diseases of cancer, arthritis, paralysis, heart disease, diabetes, etc. It is the same old Pharaoh ruling and governing us. People are groaning for deliverance.

We must enthrone in our mind spiritual values and realize that the Infinite Healing Presence, when called upon, can flow through us as harmony, wholeness, beauty and perfection. In Biblical terminology, your sense of personal spiritual power will take you over the Red Sea of troubles, calming your emotions (waters), and permitting your good ideas to pass through to outward manifestation (dry ground).

Pharaoh—our own ignorance of the Divine Presence—is always pursuing us. Millions believe in all sorts of false ideas about God. These false beliefs represent Pharaoh keeping us in bondage in Egypt. Whatever you believe in holds you in bondage. For example, many subscribe to the belief in the theory of reincarnation, which teaches that you must come back again and again in many life cycles to expiate for some sins and errors of a former life.

You are dealing with a Timeless and Spaceless Being. There is neither time nor space; the God-Presence never punishes. We must forgive ourselves as God, or Infinite Life, is forever forgiving us. Anytime we deal with time and space theories and beliefs, we are no longer in Truth. . . . *Today shalt thou be with me in paradise* (Luke 23:43). Not tomorrow, but now—today. God is the Eternal Now!

Change the beginning and you change the end. Murderers may change in the twinkling of an eye; the past is forgotten and remembered no more. A man may have been a thief, swindler and robber; now he is honest and upright and leading a new life. He does not have to suffer for errors in the past, no more so than does the man who made all kinds of blunders in mathematics but now uses the principles of mathematics the right way. The principles of mathematics have no grudge against him, and he is not penalized because he previously misused the principles. We must eradicate from our mind the false belief in the automatic weary round of rebirths, refleshing ourselves in the menial garments of the slave to carnal, materialistic thinking and living. When you rise in consciousness to the point where you forgive yourself and cleanse your mind and heart, the past is forgotten and remembered no more.

Karma and What It Means to the Scientific Thinker

Karma, or reaping what you have sown, turns out to be inexorable only as long as you do not pray or meditate on the Truths of God. As soon as you pray scientifically, you rise above karma, and the unpleasant consequences of past mistakes begin to be wiped out. No matter how awful the crime—be it murder or any other heinous offense—it can be expunged from the mind altogether with all the punishment that would ordinarily follow. The mere reading of affirmations and perfunctory prayers will not change matters. A deep hunger and thirst to become a new person in God's love and grace, plus an intense desire to transform, is essential to wipe out the punishment that must otherwise follow negative and destructive thinking.

Emma Curtiss Hopkins, author of *Higher Mysticism* and other books, tells of a wonderful event recorded in the archives of a state penal institution. This is the essence of it: A man was sentenced about eighty years ago to be hanged. In the interim between his sentence and its time of fulfillment, he sought the Face of God, which means the Truth about God. If I look at your face I recognize you. Face is, therefore, a symbol for the recognition that God is love and there is no condemnation, as God does not judge or condemn any person. *For the Father judgeth no man, but hath committed all judgment unto the Son* (John

5:22). You are the son, which also means your mind, and you are always judging yourself by the concepts and beliefs you entertain. You are always choosing thoughts, thereby passing judgment on yourself.

The murderer of whom Emma Hopkins spoke had read that "God was the bad man's deliverer," and this man had committed the murder for which he was sentenced. He accepted and believed what he read. To the great confusion and perplexity of the officers of the law, when the man was led to the gallows, however, the platform which would tip ordinarily at the slightest weight became firm the moment the condemned man stepped upon it. They tried again and again to hang him but to no avail; finally he was given his freedom.

The efficacy of his High Watch on the goodness and love of God neutralized the so-called karma of the ordinarily mandated treadmill of cause and effect, which enabled this murderer to step off into a new order of emancipated consciousness and experience. The wonders and blessings of the Infinite know no limit.

Why Do I Do This?

This was a question recently asked me by a professional man. He was what he termed a confirmed alcoholic. He would go on binges for a week or two weeks at a time. "When drunk," he said, "I'm a king for the day, but when the drunken stupor wears off,

I am despondent, gloomy and full of despair and hopelessness."

In talking with him, I found that he had a brilliant education and background and was a research adviser to a very large pharmaceutical organization. He said to me, "They praise me, but I don't feel I'm worthy of praise. I feel rotten inside. I feel I'm nobody. When I was younger, my father used to tell me I was stupid and that I would never amount to anything; he criticized me at every turn."

This man was resentful and hateful toward his father, and he had a deep sense of inferiority and insecurity. He acknowledged that alcohol was what he termed the "false spirit" which brought about oblivion for a time and banished his sense of guilt and inadequacy.

He decided to try the true Spirit, Which is God within him, Which would bring about a true exhilaration from the depths of himself. Accordingly, I gave him a spiritual formula upon which he was to reflect and meditate. I explained to him that as he practiced it faithfully, the dominant idea of peace and sobriety would take charge of his conscious mind, thereby impregnating his subconscious and eradicating his sense of inferiority and inadequacy.

Every morning and evening he practiced looking in the mirror and affirmed out loud slowly, feelingly and knowingly: "I am a son of the Living God. God's peace, harmony and joy flow through me. I am happy, joyous and free. I am inspired from On High.

God loves me and cares for me. God is working wonders and miracles in my life now." He repeated this prayer over and over again night and morning, until finally it had all the tones of reality. In about two weeks he became completely free and at peace. He proved to himself that he could rise above the sorrows of life and release the imprisoned splendor within him.

The Bible says: . . . *I bare you on eagles' wings, and brought you unto myself* (Exodus 19:4). The eagle soars aloft above the storms, typhoons and monsoons and sits still and gazes into the sun. The eagle is the only bird that soars above all storms and gazes directly into the sun. This is why the eagle was chosen by the mystics who wrote and created the great seal of the United States, and which is to remind all of us in time of trouble to look to God and pray for peace and harmony.

Likewise, this man with the wings of thought, feeling, faith and imagination rose above the storm in his own life and looked to God for freedom and peace of mind. He realized that alcohol, like Valium and other drugs, suppressed his self-condemnation and criticisms for a while, but this procedure was no nourishment for his mind and body.

Listen to the Voice Within

There is that within you that always urges you forward. It is the Life-Principle, Whose tendency is lifeward. The Bible says: *If I had not come and spoken unto them, they had not had sin: but now they have no cloak for their sin* (John 15:22). To sin is to miss the mark; it is your failure to lead a full and happy life. If ill, you are missing the mark of wholeness and vitality. If impoverished, you are missing the mark in failing to accept God's riches, which are all around you. A primitive person living in the jungle has no inner quarrel in his mind. He is satisfied and has no sin. A missionary comes along, however, and builds a cabin to protect himself from the inclemencies of the season. The primitive man becomes aware of something better and, of course, immediately wants it. He is no longer satisfied and no longer at peace.

The Life-Principle in you is forever urging you forward, telling you to rise, transcend, grow, come up higher; I have need of you. The Spirit in you is always reminding you that there is a better way of life. If you are sick, there is the Almighty One within you that reminds you that you should be well. In life you are aware of comparisons, contrasts and differences, such as colors. You would not know what light is unless you could experience darkness. If weak, there is that within you that tells you that you can become strong and powerful. If you were not now aware of the possibility of a grander, nobler and more wonderful life, you would be satisfied the way you are.

A businessman who attends my lectures, recently had some trouble with his car. He said to himself, "I am going to buy a Rolls Royce." He began to claim it. In his imagination he drove it to church and to business every day. By dramatizing the scene over and over again several times a day for some weeks, the opportunity finally came to him in a wonderful way. He saw something better than the car he had. His sin would be the failure to achieve his goal. There was a time when he would not even think of a Rolls Royce, but he had grown inwardly, spiritually and mentally; and as you grow inwardly, you grow outwardly along all lines, financially, socially, professionally and in all phases of your life.

She Said, "I'm Not Satisfied with What I Am"

A talented young musician said to me that she was content and happy in her home and work but that she wanted and desired to express herself musically at far higher levels. She began to claim frequently that God is the Great Musician and that she is expressing more and more of heavenly music every day of her life. She has gone up the ladder of life at this writing and is much happier, knowing there is no end to the heights to which she can climb. She was content and happy in her home, but not with what she was expressing.

She Said, "He Is Mean and Contemptible"

A divorcee recited all the mean, nasty and contemptible acts of her ex-husband. You become aware of these qualities and acts of the other person because the One Altogether Beautiful and Good is within you, Emerson says in *The Oversoul.* We grant that human life is mean, but how did we find out that it was mean? What is the ground for this uneasiness of ours? of this old discontent? What is the universal sense of want and ignorance but the fine innuendo by which the soul makes its enormous claims?

You know and recognize hate because Divine love indwells you, reminding you it is wrong to hate. You know it is wrong to steal because Absolute Honesty is also within you. You know it is wrong to demean yourself or others because there is that within you which reminds you that you are a son or daughter of the Infinite and a child of Eternity. You are aware of these negative passions and emotions in yourself and others, but in exalting the Divine Presence within you and in becoming aware of your Divine dignity and prerogatives, you are able to balance the opposites within you and establish equilibrium and peace of mind. You begin to understand why people act the way they do, as they are driven by negative emotions and you gradually become more tolerant and look at the experience with a greater degree of equanimity.

. . . Fear of the Lord, that Is Wisdom . . . (Job 28:28)

When the Bible was translated into English, the word *fear* at that time meant to have a healthy, reverent, wholesome respect for the Lord, or the Law, in the same way that you would have a healthy respect for the principles of chemistry or electricity. Likewise, you should have a healthy respect for your consciousness, which is the only creative power you know. Your state of consciousness is the way you think, feel, believe and what you give mental consent to. In other words, your consciousness at this moment is the sum total of your conscious and subconscious impressions, acceptances and beliefs—good or bad. There is no other creative power. You should, therefore, have a very high regard for the power of your consciousness.

A man employed generating nuclear energy at one of the numerous modern installations has a healthy concern for the proper use of this power. Naturally, he would fear a nuclear explosion. This type of fear is good, for it causes him to take wise and proper precautions in handling this dynamic force. The electrician studies the laws of conductivity and insulation and the fact that the energy flows from a higher to a lower potential, but he has no morbid fear of it. He learns to use the principles of electricity wisely.

Respect your thoughts and your mental attitude, because whatever you really believe—good or bad—will come to pass. If fear-thoughts come to you, remember that they come to everybody. You do not get a sledgehammer and try to kill them. All you do is practice the law of substitution, such as affirming, "God's love fills my soul," or "God is with me." Or, quote a verse from the 23rd Psalm, . . . *I will fear no evil: for thou art with me* . . . (Psalm 23:4). Immediately the fear goes away. Remember, you can't think of two things at the same time. Keep on supplanting the fear-thought with the spiritual thought, and after awhile, the fear-thought stops coming to your mind.

She Pretended to Be Sick

Recently I talked with a mother who said that she had discovered that her daughter would feign great pains and sickness, and on several occasions the medical doctor had said there was absolutely nothing wrong with her. In talking with the young girl I discovered that she got little or no attention from her father and mother. The mother was involved in politics a lot and her father travelled constantly in his business and had little or no time for his daughter. She admitted that she pretended to be ill and to suffer great pains in order to get attention and sympathy. She informed the author that that was the only time she received any kindness or special attention.

This girl was experiencing a sense of rejection and felt unloved and unappreciated, pointing out that in actual fact she excelled in her school life. The parents saw the point and did the commonsense thing. They explained to her that she was loved and appreciated, and they gave her more attention, taking her on trips and praising her for her wonderful school work.

Occasionally you read in the newspapers about some criminal who is delighted when he sees a write-up about himself in the newspapers. He gets a lot of attention, all based on his deep sense of insecurity, inadequacy and self-loathing. In other words, he gets attention the wrong way.

Get a New Estimate

Remember who you are. Realize that you are a son or daughter of the Infinite. Every day of your life exalt God in the midst of you. Appraise yourself from a spiritual standpoint and realize that all the powers and wonders of God are within you, waiting for you to call on the Infinite, Which always responds.

Job said: *I put on righteousness, and it clothed me: my judgment was as a robe and a diadem* (Job 29:14). Righteousness is to think right, feel right, act right and do right according to the Golden Rule and the law of love. In other words, think, speak and act from the Divine Center, and not from the superimposed structure of fear, ignorance and superstition.

The judgment is your own conclusion in your mind. You are always judging in your mind, separating falsity from Truth. Your judgment from now on is that you will see peace where discord is, love where hatred is, joy where sadness is, light where darkness is, and life where so-called death is. You will see wholeness and vitality where sickness is and God's riches where poverty is. You will begin to see others as they ought to be—happy, joyous and free.

The answer to all weakness, shyness, inferiority and the sense of inadequacy is to follow the injunction of Paul: *Wherefore I put thee in remembrance that thou stir up the gift of God, which is in thee . . .* (II Timothy 1:6).

CHAPTER 9

The Wonderful Meaning of the Morning Star

I Jesus have sent mine angel to testify unto you these things in the churches. I am the root and the offspring of David, and the bright and morning star (Revelation 22:16).

One of the meanings of the word Jesus is the same as that of Joshua, i.e., God is the emancipator, or God is the savior. It also means your desire. Your desire for health, happiness, peace, true expression and the abundant life is like the morning star which heralds the birth of the sun, which in turn redeems the earth from darkness and gloom and lights up the heavens with all its glory.

For example, your desire for perfect health heralds the birth of your savior, for the realization of your desire would save you from any trouble, be it what it may. Your desire is the root and the offspring of David, for David means God's love, and your desire is Life's love to express Itself through you. A seed in your hand is a promise of a harvest, but you must first deposit it in the soil. Likewise, your desire for health or any other good thing is God's promise in your heart telling you that you can rise and become that which you want to be. The bright and morning star is your inner conviction of your ability to accomplish whatever you undertake. This star, or attitude of mind, guides you and compels you to fulfill and bring forth the cherished desire of your heart.

Affirm boldly: "God gave me this desire. It is good and very good. The Infinite Spirit Which gave me the desire, idea or plan will reveal the perfect plan for its unfoldment." As you adhere to these truths, your desire will come to pass.

The Meaning of Prophecy for You

And he saith unto me, Seal not the sayings of the prophecy of this book: for the time is at hand. He that is unjust, let him be unjust still: and he which is filthy, let him be filthy still: and he that is righteous, let him be righteous still: and he that is holy, let him be holy still (Revelation 22:10–11).

You are your own prophet, because according to your belief is it done unto you. Your own inner feeling, your faith, your inner mood and expectancy determine that which is to come. Whatever you are planning for the future, you are planning it now. The future is always your present thoughts made visible. Whatever you unite with mentally and emotionally is a prophecy of that which is to come.

Be a true prophet, be a good prophet. Expect only

good fortune and good fortune shall be yours. The children of misfortune are those who ascribe power to externals, other people and the mass mind. These are the illegitimate children of the world. You must first change yourself; then your world will change. Unfortunately, man is always trying to change the other person.

Grant your relatives, friends and all other people the right to be different. Grant them their peculiarities, idiosyncrasies and religious viewpoints. Permit them to worship differently from yourself. Be glad there are Catholics, Jews, Protestants and Buddhists, as well as followers of other religions. If the other person is mean and nasty, that is no reason why you should be, also. You are here to let your light so shine before men that they will see your good works and recognize you as being a good example to all.

Spend some time every day radiating the glory, beauty and love of God, and never mind whether the other fellow does it or not. You are not responsible if some friend of yours shoots his or her spouse. All you are responsible for is the way you think about him or her. Since your thought is creative, you will therefore bless both, realizing that the journey of the deceased person is ever onward, upward and Godward and that the light of God shines in the person who committed the act.

There is no death; there is only Life. If someone wants to make you feel guilty because a president was assassinated, you know that that hypnotic suggestion does not apply to you. There is no end to the glory which is man, and the journey into the next dimension must be one of growth, expansion and progression along all lines. It is wrong to permit others to make you feel guilty; if you allow that, such people can manipulate your mind and you no longer own your own mind.

Change yourself, and while you are changing your world will magically mold itself in the image and likeness of your concept of yourself. Identify yourself with the lovely, and you will be unable to see the unlovely. As your eyes are identified with beauty, you cannot see the ugly things in life. Fill your mind with Divine love, and you will then discover that love transcends all creeds and dogmas.

For I testify unto every man that heareth the words of the prophecy of this book, If any man shall add unto these things, God shall add unto him the plagues that are written in this book: And if any man shall take away from the words of the book of this prophecy, God shall take away his part out of the book of life, and out of the holy city, and from the things which are written in this book (Revelation 22:18–19).

It is absolutely absurd to take these statements literally. First of all, the Bible was not written in English. You must become aware of the figurative, allegorical and metaphorical meaning of these verses. It is interesting to note that in connection with these two verses of the Bible, reference is made to the literary vandalism which was rampant in the days when the books of the Bible were written. It was customary to write them on parchment in the form of scrolls; however, religious bigots and other unscrupulous persons often changed and expunged words and passages by interpolating forgeries. The letters of Paul and other parts of the New Testament are known to have been mutilated in this manner, but Bible scholars, philologists and other research specialists know where these forgeries are.

There is no doubt but that religious sectarians were prevented from interfering with the contents of the book of Revelation inasmuch as they took the Bible literally, not realizing that its hidden meaning is actually the meat of the whole message. It is generally agreed that the text of this book of the Bible has been preserved intact through the centuries due to the fear of what men believed to be an imprecation. That is only the outer coat. The real meaning is something else altogether.

The Meaning of Your Word or The Word

Your word is your idea, thought or formulated desire. Like a seed, it has its own method of expression or manifestation. Your desire for wealth is a prophecy of that which is to come in the same way that a seed is a promise of a harvest. Your desire for health, peace, true expression or prosperity is the voice or urge of the Divine Presence in you telling you that you can not only become healthy but also have all these other things.

This is how man *adds* to the word of God: he prays for wealth and affirms that God is his Source of supply and that God's riches are circulating in his life now. A few minutes later he begins to wonder how, when, where and through what source his supply will come. He doesn't trust the Divine Source and tries to help God out. Man must learn that the ways of the Infinite Spirit are past finding out and that the Infinite Presence has countless channels. Man's prayer may be answered in countless ways and in a manner that he knoweth not, and in an hour that he expecteth not.

You Must Believe What You Affirm

Some time ago, I talked with a man who was constantly praying for prosperity and looking to God as the real Source, but at the same time he was deeply resenting his employer because he did not give him an increase in salary. This man did not believe what he was affirming. Actually, he was praying two ways and, like a soldier marking time, he was not getting anyplace. This man was double-minded and had a double allegiance. You must come to a clear-cut decision and know that God or Infinite Spirit is the Source of all our blessings and believe in your heart that whatever we claim to be true, Spirit will respond, for It is all things to all men.

Cease Adding to the Word

The Creative Principle, or God, can prosper in us in the same manner that It grows hair on your head or creates a blade of grass. It is all-wise and has the "know-how" of accomplishment. For example, a man desires promotion; this desire is good and very good. Life is growth, and his desire for advancement and expansion is the cosmic urge within him telling him to rise, transcend, grow and express himself at higher levels.

This is how he adds to the word: He looks around him and says, "Well, that fellow is going to pass on some day and I'll get that position." The desire was good, but he contaminated and adulterated it. He should know that Infinite Intelligence within him can create another position like it and one even far better. You don't want another person's job; you may desire a position like it, though, with the same prestige, salary, etc.

Infinite Intelligence has countless ways of bringing your request to pass. You don't have to hurt a hair of a living being to get ahead in life. You must never undermine or hurt another in order to achieve your goal in life. To harm another in this way would be *adding* to the word, and *God shall add unto him the plagues that are written in this book,* which means that when you hurt another, you are also hurting yourself. Whenever you use the law negatively, you will reap the results, such as neuroses, frustrations, sickness, lack and limitation.

Taking Away from The Word

You *take* from the word or the cherished desire of your heart when you say, "I can't be that" or "I can't accomplish or achieve my goal." You are actually denying the Presence and Power of God, saying that God can't fulfill His promise.

Recently a man said to me that his boy suffered from a disease that was incurable. I pointed out to him that what he was really saying was that God couldn't heal the boy. He was shocked at his own statement and in an about-face began to affirm that the Infinite Healing Presence Which created his son could certainly restore him to harmony, health and strength. Gradually a perfect healing took place, curing the blood disorder which had afflicted the boy.

A man came to see me about his son, who wanted to go to college to learn to become a physician; but the father said that he didn't have the money and that his boy was terribly depressed. The boy, in the meantime, compromised and went to work behind the soda fountain in a drug store, becoming frustrated and unhappy. The father was taking from the word of God, saying, "God could not open up the way for my boy to become a physician, so I'll get him a job somewhere." The plague that follows this attitude of mind is the failure to realize the desire of the heart, which is the cause of endless frustration and misery in the world.

The father changed his attitude and began to pray that Infinite Spirit would open up the way for his son to go to college, and he began to picture in his mind prior to sleep and at other times his son showing him his medical diploma, which stated that he had graduated as a physician and surgeon. His father kept picturing this diploma and praying for guidance and right action. In a few weeks' time an aunt of his son passed on to the next dimension and bequeathed a large estate with ample funds for his son's education.

The Fragrance Lingers

Dr. Helena Davis, who lectures for me occasionally, phoned me this morning and said her living room is full of flowers of all kinds, sent to her by loving friends. One woman had attached a note to the basket of flowers saying that the fragrance of these flowers lingers with her also. The good you do returns to you in ways you know not of. When they sent flowers, it made each one happy; therefore, they were also blessing themselves.

Let the Morning Star Rise in You

When you say "I AM," you are referring to the God-Presence within you, Which is the Living Spirit Almighty. That is the Lord of all. When you realize that your own I AMness is the Lord God Almighty, and when you recognize It as the only Presence and Power, while at the same time recognizing that the Spirit within you is your boss, your guide, your way-shower, your paymaster, your counsellor as well as the Source of all your blessings, then you are becoming aware of the morning star, Biblically speaking.

The Bible uses metaphors and figures of speech to illustrate the invisible powers within you. The morning star comes into your experience when you become aware of God within you; then you are able to cast light upon your problems and rise to great heights along all lines.

He Shoots the Stars

There are stars of truth within you just as there are stars in the heavens above. A captain on the plane to Tokyo told me that sometimes his plane is caught in a great storm; then he "shoots the stars" and gets a reference point. In other words, he said that with his instrument he gets a "fix" on a certain star, and from that angle he can calculate his exact position.

In a similar manner, when you have a difficult problem turn your eyes to the Divine Presence within and affirm boldly, "God knows the answer and I give thanks for the answer now."

In Greenwich Observatory, the positions of the stars and the sun are calculated in order to get the exact time. The stars were the first clocks and calendars of the ancient seers and mystics, who noticed that at certain seasons of the year beneficial changes on earth coincided with astronomical changes in the heavens. So, in a sense, the stars were the first calendars. The earth moving around the sun caused the ancients to become aware of spring, summer, autumn and winter. The apparent movement of the stars was really due to the orbital movement of the earth. The ancient mystics knew that the stars were revolving also; they had no instruments that we know of, but undoubtedly they had an intuitive perception.

The morning star heralds the dawn or the birth of the sun, which spreads its glorious rays over the heavens and all darkness disappears. When the sun crosses the equator in the spring, all nature is resurrected and the desert rejoices and blossoms as the rose. This is why the sun in its northern journey was called the savior of the world. It is darkest before the dawn, and when the sun appears all nature rejoices. The sun was a symbol for God among ancient people. They knew it was not God, but its movements and functions were Godlike insofar as all life on earth was concerned.

She Discovered the Light Within

A woman living here in Leisure World told me that she was in the depths of despair. She had just received a diagnosis of a hopeless, terminal case of cancer, considered inoperable because it had metastasized to such a great extent. She called it her darkest night. She said that all night long she claimed out loud, "The light of God shines in my whole being." Finally, she fell into a sound sleep, however, and a saintly figure appeared to her, saying, "You are healed."

She realized that this undoubtedly was a revelation to her from her deeper mind, and she intuitively knew that she was healed. Her physician confirmed the healing, referring to it as a spontaneous remission. The answer came to her as she turned with faith and confidence to the Light within, which cast out all the darkness in her subconscious mind. She had discovered the morning star within herself.

Her awareness of the Healing Light was the star that heralded the dawn in her life. God created the stars and the whole world. Symbolically, the stars of God are the stars of truth, light, love and wisdom, which light up the heavens of our mind and give us peace, poise, equanimity and serenity. To many aerial navigators, poets and writers, the stars represent a matchless source of inspiration and encouragement. In all Scriptures light is a common symbol for Truth, as darkness represents false beliefs and errors in the mind.

The Light of the Body Is the Eye

The light of the body is the eye: if therefore thine eye be single, thy whole body shall be full of light. But if thine eye be evil, thy whole body shall be full of darkness. If therefore the light that is in thee be darkness, how great is that darkness! (Matthew 6:22–23).

The eye, symbolically speaking, means spiritual perception. You might ask: How can light be darkness? False information, wrong concepts of God and superstitious beliefs represent darkness or ignorance. Millions believe many things about Life which are absolutely false. These beliefs in the subconscious mind of the masses bring forth all manner of troubles, sickness, lack and limitation.

The sun in you means your awareness of the Presence and Power of God within you. The Son, or sun, means that you can express here and now the wisdom, the power and the glory of the Infinite by turning within and claiming boldly that all that is true of God is true of you. As you make a habit of this, these truths will revolve in the heavens of your mind and appear on your earth, i.e., your body, your business, your home, your expression and all phases of your life. Remember this simple and very practical truth: Whatever you focus your attention on is the thing that governs your life.

You have heard many times that attention is the key to life. Ask yourself this question: How am I directing my attention now? Spiritual-minded people steadfastly direct their attention to God, realizing that God is their guide, counsellor, paymaster and the Source of health, wealth and all the blessings of life. They give no attention or power to externals, other people or conditions. They give power to the Creator and not to the created thing. Millions of people do not direct their attention to spiritual principles. They are governed by mass propaganda, traditional beliefs, etc. They are like drifting logs in the sea, tossed to and fro, double-minded and unstable in all their ways. This attitude on the part of so many people brings on poverty, misery, ill health and all sorts of trouble.

Put God first in your life and realize that you are a son or daughter of the Infinite and a child of Eternity and that God flows through you as harmony, beauty, love, peace and joy. When God, or the Living Spirit, in your life is in complete charge and governing your entire life, your eye is single and your whole body, or embodiment, will be full of light, love, truth and beauty.

You Can Find Yourself Now

The real you is the I AM in you, which is God. It is the only creative power. It is all there is, for there is nothing but God and His countless manifestations.

A young girl who had a beautiful voice wanted to be recognized and express her talents. She pictured herself singing beautifully before an audience, and she heard her teacher congratulating her. She practiced this over and over again until the private movie of her mind had all the tones of reality. At the time of this writing, she has appeared again and again before social groups as the major attraction. She created according to the image and likeness of her thoughts. The cause was her own consciousness, which means the way she thought, felt and imaged.

The Cause of all creation is the Spirit in you. You are sovereign over your world. You are also in charge of your relationships with other people. Darkness is here so that we may appreciate the light; poverty or lack is present so that we may learn and experience the fullness and abundance of God in the land of the living. The primitive man living in the jungles (and some people are still living in the Stone Age) may have never seen a home in his life and is satisfied with his lot. But when some missionary builds a hut for himself to protect him from the inclemencies of the seasons, the primitive man becomes aware of something better. How would you know what joy was unless you could shed a tear of sorrow? Your problems and difficulties enable you to discover the Divinity within you.

She Ceased Condemning Herself

Recently I counselled a woman who had just been married. She had committed murder in another state and had served time; she was full of self-condemnation and guilt. She was also full of fear of being exposed, as she moved in very high professional circles.

I explained to her that the very first thing she must do was to cease condemning herself. Whenever the guilt or fear-thought came to her mind, she should supplant it immediately with, "I am a daughter of God. God loves me and cares for me." I added that as she keeps this up, the day will come when she will be completely at peace. I advised her not to fight the thought of self-condemnation but to supplant it with the God-like thought and that after awhile the subconscious is reconditioned. Even if she went back to the town where the crime occurred, the accusers and the wagging tongues of the gossips would cease to be. The reason is that when you stop accusing yourself, others stop accusing and vilifying you.

She began to see that the Real Self of her was God, and that it was the false self, or the malconditioned self, that had committed the crime. She was, of course, responsible for her act and had served time in prison as punishment for it for many years. The point is that she no longer has to browbeat herself and torture herself mentally. God never punishes; all of us punish ourselves by our misuse of the Laws of Life and the way of the Infinite Spirit. She practiced that simple truth and is now radiating the sunshine of God's love.

Don't Let Others Manipulate Your Mind

I visited Germany, Switzerland and England last year and gave a series of lectures in the major cities.

In Germany one of the teachers told me that he had heard of an ex-convict in Holland who became friends with a carpenter. This carpenter was an honest and upright man and also very religious. It seems that the ex-convict had hypnotized him several times, suggesting each time to him that he should get a gun, hold up a certain bank and bring him the bag of money. These hypnotic suggestions were repeated frequently to the carpenter, gradually breaking down his sense of honesty and integrity and reconditioning his subconscious with the diabolical suggestion to rob the bank.

One day he went to the particular bank with a gun, demanded the money, and in the scuffle that followed, he shot the teller and was eventually brought up on first degree murder charges. A court psychiatrist rehypnotized the carpenter and got the answer, because the carpenter, under hypnosis, revealed word for word the suggestions given to him by the ex-convict. The latter was later sentenced and the carpenter set free.

Many people with their eyes wide open are being similarly hypnotized by false ideas. For instance, they believe that others can mar their happiness and hurt them by such things as voodoo practices. Others believe they are victims of karma and are placed here on earth to suffer and expiate for past crimes. Countless people are full of a myriad of religious prejudices and hatreds, and many even kill each other in the name of religion. These are suggestions and lies repeated over and over again, and many who have no spiritual awareness accept these lies as truth, bringing misery and suffering in their train.

Reject any teaching which holds you in bondage and which teaches fear or limits or inhibits you in any way. No one can imprison you if you live in freedom in God and His love. No one can steal your days and nights from you or deprive you of wealth, health or happiness unless you first steal from yourself. The angel unlocked the cell of Peter and set him free. Likewise, as you rise to the conviction of your Divine freedom, the angel of your Higher-Self, which is your conviction of God's Presence, will open the prison doors for you and set you free to practice the Presence of God.

How to Become Sons of God

When we are imbued with lofty ideals and when we think Godlike thoughts, unpleasant little things disappear and all the petty things of life become inconsequential and are forgotten. Our soul actually becomes filled with the glory of the whole, and the limitations and restrictions of our daily life vanish. We find that this happy mood lifts us up and brings us *en rapport* with the Universal mind of God.

As greed, jealousy, discord and other narrowing concepts which bind us to the wheel of pain disappear from our consciousness, forgotten in the joy of Truth, we no longer are sons of man, but we become sons of God. We become one with the universal vistas. Constant meditation, either in the woods, in your own home or wherever you may be, causes your soul to thrill as if touched by a Divine harmony, and a pulsating, throbbing feeling pervades every part of you. It is as if the melody of the gods were played on your heartstrings.

In conclusion, let us contemplate this profound truth: *Beloved, now are we the sons of God, and it doth not yet appear what we shall be: but we know that, when he shall appear, we shall be like him; for we shall see him as he is* (I John 3:2).

CHAPTER 10

Therapy for Loneliness

Emerson said: "If you want a friend, be a friend." As you know, there is a law of attraction in this universe, and this law, properly used, does attract friends. Your subconscious mind* will respond according to the ideas you impress upon it. It is a law of reflection. An old saying is as follows: "Life is the mirror of king or slave." Whatever you predominantly think and believe will be produced by your subconscious on the screen of space. In other words, your subconscious responds to your belief and your own evaluation of yourself.

She Was Lonesome

A girl from Texas obtained a position in a large office in Los Angeles. She had no friends and felt very lonesome. She said to me, "I never have a date. No one pays any attention to me." I explained to her that her subconscious mind takes her literally and responds accordingly.

*See *The Power of Your Subconscious Mind* by Dr. Joseph Murphy, Prentice-Hall, Inc., Englewood Cliffs, New Jersey, 1963.

I suggested to her that she begin to image ideal relationships and sense and feel the presence of friends, both men and women. As a result she began to practice the following prayer: "Infinite Intelligence attracts to me wonderful friends who are spiritually oriented and who harmonize with me perfectly. I radiate love, peace, joy and goodwill to all the men and women in my office and to all people everywhere. I give thanks for the joy of the answered prayer." She kept repeating this prayer, knowing that by repetition, faith, and expectancy, she was writing her request into her subconscious mind.

Shortly afterwards, a girl in the office invited her to a Science of Mind church, where she met a host of friends and subsequently married a business executive who also attended the same lectures and classes she had been attending. She discovered that the law of attraction works.

All of us possess a subconscious mind which is one with the universal subconscious mind. It is receptive, impersonal, always receiving the impression of our thoughts, thus creating the things and circumstances which we think upon.

Getting in Touch with Subconscious Mind

The right direction is to be found in the impersonal quality of your subconscious mind. That is to say, not impersonal as lacking the elements of personality, but impersonal in the sense of not recognizing the particular external relations which appear to the conscious or objective mind. Your subconscious acts deductively and can overcome any external handicap or problem.

A widow living here in Laguna Hills, California, told me that she had four children and was employed by the government. But she had told herself that no man wanted to be saddled with her four children and that, therefore, she could not attract a marriageable man. She failed to see that her subconscious mind reasons deductively only and is noncontroversial. It accepted what she decreed. While many men in her office took her to lunch and dinner occasionally, no one ever asked her to marry him.

She reversed her mental attitude. The process consisted in first forming a clear conception of the idea she wished to convey to her subconscious mind, and then mentally addressing her subconscious mind and impressing upon it what she really wanted. She formulated her own technique, which was very simple and effective: "I am happily married to a wonderful and loving man who loves me and my children. I decree this, I mean it, and I know you will bring it to pass." In the morning she would silently repeat the same request, making sure that she did not contradict during the day what she had previously affirmed. She committed to her subconscious mind its task in full confidence that, by the law of its nature, it would do so if not hindered by a repetition of contrary messages from her conscious mind.

Her supervisor, with whom she had worked for five years, and who had never even asked her for a date, suddenly asked her to marry him. She said that at first she was flabbergasted, and then realized that it was an answer to her prayer and she readily accepted.

It has been shown both by theory and practice that such is the law of the relation between the subconscious and conscious mind. You will find yourself face to face with a modus operandi which brings to fulfillment the desires of your heart.

She Had a Friend

Recently I conducted a memorial service for a woman who had passed on in a nursing home. Apparently, at one time she had been very rich but had lost everything. Her family never visited her, and there was only one person at the memorial service—a young woman who said that the deceased had been very good to her when she had been down and out. She had given her a job, had bought her a car, and had sent her to college, all at her own expense. She said to me, "This is what I want to do: To have this memorial in honor of the greatest friend I have ever had."

Now this is real friendship, and you can see that it penetrated to the depths of this young woman's subconscious mind. The deceased was obviously outgoing, generous and kind. The lonely person is usually ingoing or wrapped up mentally and emotionally in his or her loneliness.

You Can Overcome Loneliness

Remember, you are living in a subjective and objective world. You must learn to balance the two and lead a full and happy life. The bird lives in the air for only a limited period of time, but then it must come down to earth to get food and procreate. The bird leads a balanced life. You are also here to express yourself and give of your talents to the world and to be amiable, sociable and kind, because nature abhors extremes of any kind.

He Was a Chronic Pessimist

A man came to me for consultation. He had lost a fairly good position and his third wife had walked out and obtained a divorce. He was very depressed and was obviously all wrapped up in himself and his troubles. He was looking at the dark side of everything: "The country is going to the dogs, the politicians are all crooks, our money is not going to be worth anything. Women are no good; all they want is money, and all of them run around. I never get the breaks; I am always the first one to be laid off the job. A jinx seems to be following me." In addition, his health was bad, and he owed a lot of money.

I asked him why his third wife had divorced him, and his answer was that she said he was too negative and that she couldn't take it any longer. Oftentimes, though, the explanation is the cure. I explained to him that he can no more have prosperity than he can have health or peace of mind with the mental attitude he had framed for himself and that he, himself, was his greatest enemy.

He began to realize that he had been misusing and misdirecting his subconscious mind and had brought on himself all his accumulated troubles and losses. This is the meaning of that remarkable passage in the Bible: *With the pure thou wilt shew thyself pure; and with the froward thou wilt shew thyself froward* (Psalm 18:26), for the content makes it clear that these words are addressed to the Divine Being. It is the unvarying law of the subconscious mind that whatever is impressed upon it, good or bad, will become objective correspondences. Natural laws admit of no exceptions.

He practiced regularly the following prayer, which changed his life and his relationships with others:

"Today is God's day. I choose happiness, success, prosperity, and peace of mind. I am Divinely guided all day long, and whatever I do will prosper. Whenever my attention wanders away from my thoughts of success, peace, prosperity, or my good, I will immediately bring back my thoughts to the contemplation of God and His love, knowing that He careth for me.

"I am a spiritual magnet, attracting to myself customers and clients who want what I have to offer. I give better service every day. I am a wonderful success in all my undertakings. I bless and prosper all those who come into my store. All these thoughts are now sinking into my subconscious mind, and they come forth as abundance, security, and peace of mind. It is wonderful!"

She Learned to Lead a Balanced Life

While speaking in Atlanta recently, a young woman was brought to my attention who was all wrapped up in metaphysics, Bible studies and meditative techniques. She had a brilliant background from an academic standpoint, but was so involved subjectively that she was careless about her work, her dress and her family and was living within herself. She was beginning to be lopsided, unbalanced, and appeared to be a sort of a strange, "cultish" figure.

I explained to her that a true knowledge of the laws of mind and the way of the Spirit would cause her to take far more interest in her teaching work and in her relations with the students and members of her own family. The inside world is the world of causes, and those causes are always expressed outwardly as results. There is a time for meditation, prayer, and study of spiritual processes, but you must also live fully in the objective sphere of life. Likewise, the man or woman who becomes all absorbed in the objective side of life and pays no attention to the spiritual world of cause within himself will inevitably become lopsided and unbalanced, as well as subject to the mass or irrational mind, called the law of averages, and, of course, will suffer accordingly.

I told this teacher who had consulted me to take up dancing and golf, to go out and meet people, and to be gracious, amiable, sociable and exude vibrancy and good humor. She had no boyfriends, which was abnormal, and she did not swim, dance, play cards or hike. She was all wrapped up in her books and was suffering as a result from religious indigestion.

She decided to follow these suggestions and to release constructively the inner splendor which she possessed. According to a letter I recently received from her, she has met a doctor on the golf course and has fallen in love with him. It is true that nature abhors extremes.

The Benign Father

Jesus, in speaking to the unlearned but fascinated audiences, told them to picture to themselves God, or the Living Spirit Almighty, in all of us as a benign Father, tenderly compassionate toward all, and sending the common bounties of nature alike on the good and the evil. He said that the sun shines on the just and the unjust, the rain falls on the good and the evil, obviously pointing out to them the impersonal nature of the Law. Prayer was to be made to this Divine

Being, not with doubt, fear, begging and beseeching, but with the absolute assurance of an answer. No limit was to be set upon Its power or willingness to respond to us. He impresses upon his listeners the exact correspondence of the attitude of this Divine Power towards them with their own attitude toward the Power.

Therefore, when you go to the subjective world of cause within you and develop an invisible movement of your mind toward your ideals, goals and solutions, your deeper mind will respond and you will experience new environmental conditions and circumstances. If lonely, remember that you are alone with your loneliness. I suggest to many elderly people here in Leisure World to join clubs, to move out among people and make friends, to enjoy some social activities, and relax and give of their talents to those around them.

Many of them who are retired began to teach, giving classes in history, German, French and other languages. Some of them became travelling companions and guides for others going to foreign countries. They acted as interpreters and had the time of their lives. There are all sorts of activities here—political, social, religious, and opportunities for people to express themselves in countless ways. One man, aged ninety, teaches lessons on bridge and has lots of friends. He says that when you drink wine you sip it slowly, and in that way you enjoy the flavor and bouquet.

Loss of Loved Ones

Tragedies, losses and disappointments come into the lives of all people. You can't keep your loved ones forever. Everyone passes on to the next dimension sooner or later. This is universal and happens to all without exception. It must be good or it would not be. The journey is from glory to glory, from octave to octave, from strength to strength, and from wisdom to higher wisdom, and so on through the currents of Eternity.

Some time ago I conducted a memorial service for the wife of a retired engineer. They had been married for over sixty years. He said he found himself catapulted into a hole of depression and a vacuum of loneliness. I asked him a very simple question: Supposing you had passed on first? How would your wife have handled it? "Oh," he said, "she would have been terribly distraught, depressed, and dejected. She couldn't take it. She would feel helpless and alone." "Well," I said, "don't you see that you saved her from that experience?"

He saw the point and realized that he was just wrapped up in his own morbidity and was feeling sorry for himself. I explained to him that love always frees the other and that he was holding his loved one back by his morbid thoughts. Protracted grief is always selfish. I suggested to him that he surrender her to God and rejoice in her new birthday, knowing that her journey is ever onward, upward and Godward; that she had met loving hands to guide her through the many mansions (dimensions) of our Father's house.

He was a deeply spiritual man and understood the entire subject. He decided that whenever she came to his mind, he would say, "I rejoice in your new birthday in God. God be with you." This benediction neutralizes all negativity, sadness and gloom. He went back to his consulting work and is now enjoying life to the fullest.

Come Out of Depression

Begin now to lift somebody else up. Be friendly; radiate love and goodwill to all those around you. Be genial, cordial, and exude vibrancy. All of these qualities are within you. All you have to do is to stir them up.

A girl who is sixteen years of age, the only daughter and apparently the only surviving relative, asked me to conduct a memorial service for her father. She was clairvoyant and said that she saw her father walking up and down, listening to what I said. She added that he smiled and wanted her to know that he was very much alive. She had been depressed, but after the service she realized there was no death.

I spoke of life, advising that so-called death was

really a new beginning. Death is ignorance, and in the Bible death means ignorance of the Truth and lack of knowledge that God is within you, the very Life of you, and that Life, or God, cannot die. The Upanishads say, "Life was never born, It will never die, water wets It not, fire burns It not, wind blows It not away. Why grievest thou for me?"

This young girl solved her depression. She said that she would make her father very happy if she studied diligently, applied herself, went to college and took up the study of medicine, as she had wanted to become a physician and her father had put aside money for her education. She knew that her success in this field would make him very happy and proud of her. This young girl thus solved her own problem and wiped away all tears.

A good cry is beneficial; it is a release. But it should not be repeated very often, as then it would become habitual and destructive. Protracted grief is always morbid selfishness and robs you of vitality, enthusiasm, and energy and brings on all manner of diseases. When you love someone who passes on, you radiate love and peace to that person. You love to see the other as he or she ought to be—happy, radiant, and advancing in the sunshine of God's love.

Blessed Be Nothing

There are many people who, when tragedy or death of a loved one takes place in their lives, go within and wallow in despondency and gloom, saying to themselves: "Blessed be nothing." It is not what happens to you that matters so much, it is your reaction to it, the way you think about it.

Recently, following one of the floods in our area of Southern California, a woman arrived at her home, which had been completely destroyed. She had lost everything, including her daughter and husband. She said to the reporters: "I have God, and God solves all problems. I go forward from here." She reacted with faith and confidence in the Only Presence and Power. With faith like that, she will climb the mountains and find ways of pleasantness and paths of peace. She knew that God indwelt her and that there was nothing lost in the Infinite.

"Open my eyes that I may see" should be our constant prayer. *The spirit of God hath made me, and the breath of the Almighty hath given me life* (Job 33:4). . . . *Let all those that put their trust in thee rejoice* . . . (Psalm 5:11). She lifted her eyes above the tragedy, knowing that what she was doing in her mind would externalize in all phases of her life. She suffered for the joy that was set before her.

The alcoholic suffers from the shakes and the jitters and agonies of withdrawal temporarily for the joy of freedom, sobriety and peace of mind which is coming to him. He knows something wonderful is working for him, and after a little while he is free. He decides to cleanse his mind of all sense of guilt, remorse and self-condemnation. As he does that, the

Holy Spirit rushes in, filling up the vacuum, and he is free. To suffer means "to allow" or "to undergo."

For whom the Lord loveth he chasteneth . . . (Hebrews 12:6). This means that if you want a healing or if you want to prosper, you must eradicate or cleanse your mind of those thought-patterns or disease-soaked images which are holding you back and preventing you from moving forward in life. If you had a bad teacher of music and you play badly, you must now discipline and school yourself to the new pattern or you cannot become a great musician.

Does Your Investment Pay Dividends?

Your thoughts and mental imagery should pay you fabulous dividends in the way of a greater measure of health, happiness, peace and abundance. Every thought is creative; therefore, you can create a far more wonderful life. Your problem of loneliness is really the result of unwise investment of your thought life. Your future is your present thinking matured or made manifest. There is no government in the world that can guarantee you perfect peace, happiness, prosperity or security. You give all these things to yourself. The only secure government is the one enthroned in your own mind, a government of Divine ideas and principles, mothered by Divine love. This is the government of the free. This government established in your conscious mind will guarantee you security, health and happiness.

As you dwell consciously on God's eternal verities, your heart will become a chalice of God's love; then all your ways will be pleasantness and all your paths will be peaceful and harmonious. The Psalmist* says: *As the hart panteth after the water brooks, so panteth my soul after thee, O God. My soul thirsteth for God, for the living God . . . Why art thou cast down, O my soul? and why art thou disquieted in me? hope thou in God: for I shall yet praise him for the help of his countenance* (Psalm 42:1,2,5).

This, Too, Will Pass Away

Everything passes away. Nothing is forever. You can't be sick forever. Everything is constantly changing. You are constantly changing. Nothing stands still. You are not the same person you were a year ago or five years ago. If you have taken up the study of the laws of mind, you have found that you don't think, speak or act the same way as formerly. You are not the same person psychologically, spiritually or physically. Science tells us that we have a new body every seven months. Realize also that everyone eventually passes on to the next dimension of life, and it is right to bless all those people, wishing them Godspeed in that journey that knows no end.

*See *Songs of God: An Interpretation of My Favorite Psalms* by Joseph Murphy, DeVorss and Company, Inc., Marina del Rey, Ca., 1979.

She Was Slowly Dying

A young woman brought her mother to see me, and in conversing with her, I found that every day she would go to the resting place of her deceased husband, carry flowers and place them on the grave, and cry for half an hour or more. Her physician had told her to stop doing this. He told her he could find nothing physically wrong with her, but she was actually pining away, and the tonic she was taking apparently had no effect.

I explained to her that in actual fact there was no one in the grave and that she was identifying with cessation, finality, death and limitation and creating the same condition in her body. I added that she should give the flowers of her heart to her deceased husband, as he was right where she was and separated by frequency only. Nobody is buried anyplace, and the markings on graves are all lies. Life is eternal and Life is progression, an endless unfoldment ever onward and upward. Life goes not backward nor tarries with yesterday. You can't be less tomorrow than you are today.

This woman had also lost a son in the Air Force during the war. He was in a combat plane. I asked her if she had gone up in the air and placed a mark there, saying that this is when he was born and this is the date he died. Of course not. Look at the thousands lost at sea during the various wars and other catastrophes. You don't go out into the ocean and place a mark there. When your electric bulb burns out, you don't say that that is the end of electricity. If a musician loses his violin, that is not the end of music. Music is. Life is. Electricity is. This woman was identifying with death and thinking of cessation and was dying inside, since you become what you contemplate.

She ceased visiting the grave and released her husband once and for all, affirming: "I surrender my husband to God completely. I radiate love, peace and joy to him. Whenever I think of him, or whenever anyone mentions him to me, I will immediately bless him, saying, 'God loves you, John. God's peace fills your soul.' "

You cannot think of two things at the same time, and as she practiced this spiritual therapy, her vision began to improve and her ophthalmologist was very pleased with her progress. Never mourn the dead; there are no dead.

An ancient poet wrote: "I said to the man who stood at the Gate of the Year, 'Give me a light that I may tread safely into the unknown.' And he replied, 'Go out into the darkness and put your hand into the hand of God. That shall be to you better than a light and safer than a known way.' "

The light, or knowledge of God, came into this woman's mind and dispelled the darkness of gloom, sorrow and depression. You come out of loneliness when you begin to emphasize in yourself the qualities of friendship, love, goodwill and a sense of humor. While you are projecting these qualities, you may still be depressed, but you have the faith to know that as you continue exuding vibrancy, goodwill, laughter, cordiality and geniality, you are building a new mental house of peace and harmony.

Invest your thoughts wisely. Rise above the problem and redeem it. Deposit faith, confidence, and trust in the law of your mind. Like the money you deposit in the bank, you will in a similar manner receive compound interest in the way of a greater measure of health, happiness, peace and prosperity. Your subconscious always magnifies what you deposit in it.

From Adversity, Many Find Strength

The following articles appeared in the *Los Angeles Times,* December 7 and 8, 1980, in the "Dear Abby" column and are self-explanatory:

> "Dear Abby: Twenty years ago, at the age of 40, I became totally disabled due to a brain tumor. I wasn't able to get out of bed, but by the grace of God and a surgeon's skill, I made it. At times I was so despondent I prayed it would all end. Then a friend gave me the enclosed inspirational piece, which I must have read 1,000 times. I had moments when

my vision clouded, and I thought, 'This is it; this is the end.' Then I'd read that message again, and it pulled me through.

"Abby, some of the greatest men and women of our times have been saddled with disabilities and adversities but have managed to overcome them.

"Perhaps somewhere among your readers there is someone who is at the end of his or her rope and needs encouragement. Pass this along. It may save a life. It saved mine.

"H.E.

"Encino, Calif.

"WINNING AGAINST THE ODDS

" 'Cripple him, and you have a Sir Walter Scott.

" 'Lock him in a prison cell, and you have a John Bunyan.

" 'Bury him in the snows of Valley Forge, and you have a George Washington.

" 'Raise him in abject poverty, and you have an Abraham Lincoln.

" 'Subject him to bitter religious prejudice, and you have a Disraeli.

" 'Afflict him with asthma as a child, and you have a Theodore Roosevelt.

" 'Stab him with rheumatic pains until he can't sleep without an opiate, and you have a Steinmetz.

"'Put him in a grease pit of a locomotive roundhouse, and you have a Walter P. Chrysler.

"'Make him second fiddle in an obscure South American orchestra, and you have a Toscanini.'

"Dear Herman: Thank you for the above. It is indeed inspirational, but I would like to add another winner to the list:

"'At birth, deny a child the ability to see, hear and speak, and you have a Helen Keller.'

"Dear Readers: Yesterday's column was filled with names (submitted by my readers) of those who managed to succeed against the odds. Today's is a continuance of that list:

"Have a thalidomide child born with a dwarfed, twisted body without arms, and you have a Terry Wiles, who, with the aid of mechanical devices, learned to play the electric organ, steer a motorboat and paint.

"Amputate the cancer-ridden leg of a handsome young Canadian, and you have a Terry Fox, who vowed to run on one leg across the whole of Canada to raise $1 million for cancer research. (Terry was forced to quit halfway when cancer invaded his lungs, but to date has raised about $20 million.)

"After having lost both legs in an air crash,

let a British fighter pilot fly again with the RAF, and you have a Douglas Bader, who, with two artificial limbs, was captured by the Germans three times during World War II—and escaped three times!

"Blind him and you have a Ray Charles, George Shearing, Stevie Wonder, Tom Sullivan, Alec Templeton or Hal Krents.

"Label him 'too stupid to learn,' and you have a Thomas Edison.

"Make him a 'hopeless' alcoholic, and you have a Bill Wilson, founder of Alcoholics Anonymous.

"Tell her she's too old to start painting at 80, and you have a Grandma Moses.

"Afflict him with periods of depression so severe that he cuts off his own ear, and you have a Vincent Van Gogh.

"Your list would not be complete without a smiling Max Cleland, who lost both legs and an arm in Vietnam and now heads the Veterans Administration in Washington, D.C.

"Don't forget Patricia Neal, the fine actress who suffered a severe stroke, but rehabilitated herself against overwhelming odds.

"Blind him at age 44, and you have John Milton, who, 16 years later, wrote 'Paradise Lost.'

"Call him dull and hopeless and flunk him

in the sixth grade, and you have a Winston Churchill.

"Punish her with poverty and prejudice, and she may survive to become another Golda Meir.

"Pit her against sexual discrimination, and you have a Madame Curie.

"Tell a young boy who loved to sketch and draw that he has no talent, and you have a Walt Disney.

"Take a crippled child whose only home he ever knew was an orphanage, and you have a James E. West, who became the first chief executive of the Boy Scouts of America.

"Rate him as 'mediocre' in chemistry, and you have a Louis Pasteur.

"Make him a homosexual, and you have a Michaelangelo and a million other talented people.

"Not all disabilities are physical and visible. And not all who have won against the odds are well-known celebrities.

"Every family has its own heroes and heroines for whom there is no medal distinguished enough to reward them for their accomplishments.

"It is to you, whose names do not appear here but deserve to, that I dedicate this column."

If our method of using our mind in the past has brought us sorrow, fear and trouble, we have only to fall back on the law that if we reverse the cause, the effects will be reversed also; and so what we have to do is simply to reverse our mental attitude and endeavor to act up to the new one, knowing that changed attitudes change everything. Remember, it is the sincere intention that is essential, and this will in time release us from the bondage and thralldom of habits which at present may seem very difficult.

Belief in limitation is the one and only thing that causes limitation, because we then impress limitation upon our subconscious mind. As we cast that belief aside and accept the life more abundant, greater and grander blessings will be ours. Never fear to be yourself. As Walt Whitman said: "You are not all included between your hat and your boots."

CHAPTER 11

Samson and Delilah

And she said unto him, How canst thou say, I love thee, when thine heart is not with me? thou hast mocked me these three times, and hast not told me wherein thy great strength lieth.

And it came to pass, when she pressed him daily with her words, and urged him, so that his soul was vexed unto death;

That he told her all his heart, and said unto her, There hath not come a razor upon mine head; for I have been a Nazarite unto God from my mother's womb: if I be shaven, then my strength will go from me, and I shall become weak, and be like any other man.

And when Delilah saw that he had told her all his heart, she sent and called for the lords of the Philistines, saying, Come up this once, for he hath shewed me all his heart. Then the lords of the Philistines came up unto her, and brought money in their hand.

And she made him sleep upon her knees; and she called for a man, and she caused him to shave off the seven locks of his head; and she began to afflict him, and his strength went from him.

And she said, The Philistines be upon thee, Samson. And he awoke out of his sleep, and said, I will go out as at other times before, and shake myself. And he wist not that the Lord was departed from him.

But the Philistines took him, and put out his eyes, and brought him down to Gaza, and bound him with fetters of brass; and he did grind in the prison house.

(Judges 16:15-21)

Samson means the sun, sunlike, sunny, distinguished. Delilah means lustful pining, poured out, exhausted, weak. She is described as a Philistine woman whom Samson loved; she was instrumental in bringing about his downfall. The name also means deceived by the five senses.

A Philistine means to deviate from the Truth, to move to and fro, and to believe in forces foreign to the Spirit, or God. Philistines were a tribe of people in Palestine that was always at enmity with the Israelites and there was constant war between them. The Philistines were opposed to all true spiritual discipline; they worshipped strange gods and resorted to all kinds of sorcery and soothsaying.

Everything in the Bible has an inner meaning. All the characters, cities, towns, animals, etc., represent states of consciousness within all of us. For example, if a man is governed by his five senses and makes no attempt to tap the God-Presence within, he is, in

Biblical language, governed by Philistine thoughts, an avalanche of sights and sounds, sundry concepts, good and bad, but mostly negative.

Israelites in the Bible represent those who give all allegiance to the One Power—God; therefore, when you read about the two armies in the Book of Samuel, Israelites and Philistines, these represent two aggregations of thought in the mind of every individual: those who know the Truth and entertain Godlike thoughts, and those whose thoughts are in open enmity and violent opposition to everything Godlike. In the inner meaning of the Bible we call these armies Truth and error. The error army in all of us seems larger and stronger, based on our early training and indoctrination. The army of Truth is made up of spiritual, invisible forces, Godlike thoughts and eternal verities.

Solar Allegories

The Bible deals with solar allegories to portray great psychological and spiritual truths. The ancient writers of the Bible were masters of allegory. The story of Samson is given in Judges, Chapters 13 to 16, inclusive. In this chapter the key verses have been set forth and they will be explained from modern-day experiences, i.e., from a psychological and spiritual standpoint.

The story of Samson, like a great many other stories in the Bible, is a concealed myth which is very similar to the Greek myth of Hercules, the Sun God. Hercules means the Sun. Samson is a solar personification and he performs the labors of Hercules. The spring equinox occurred in different signs of the Zodiac based on the procession of the equinoxes. The sun is said to be born at the winter solstice when it begins to rise in the heavens and stimulates all nature; the brown earth becomes green, the snow and ice begin to melt, and the desert rejoices and blossoms as the rose.

Samson's strength, according to the Bible, was in his seven locks of hair. Obviously, this cannot be taken literally. Hair in the Bible means spiritual power and vibrations which emanate from the Godlike person. It is easy to follow the solar allegory. The sun born at the winter solstice represents the first lock of hair; and as it gradually rises in the heavens, until it reaches the point called the summer solstice, which takes place in the sign of Leo, the Lion, figuratively speaking, the sun has traversed seven signs or possesses seven locks of hair.

Samson slew the lion, and the Bible says he found honey in the carcass. When the sun reaches the sign Leo, it is said to conquer the sign, or slay it. When the Bible says that Samson carried away the gates of Gaza, the latter word means strength, a stronghold, all of which is symbolic of the power and strength of the sun as it breaks through the gates from Pisces to Aries, called the ingress of Aries or the spring equinox.

As the sun begins to descend, the first sign it touches

is Virgo, the Virgin, which, in the solar allegory, is Delilah. Everyone knows the rays of the sun begin to decrease in intensity and light as it enters Virgo. As the sun reaches Libra, the autumnal equinox takes place and the sun descends below the equator. This is where Samson's (Sun) hair (or rays) is cut off. It is said that his two eyes are blinded, indicating loss of power and sight. Eye means spiritual perception. Finally, the sun, or Samson, is said to die, which is the winter solstice.

All the sun-gods of antiquity represent the God-Presence in all of us and, like the sun in its northern passage, save us from darkness and limitation. So also does the awareness of the God-Power within us resurrect our dead hopes, dreams and aspirations. When we allow the Spirit of God to move through our twelve faculties and discipline them, we will emancipate ourselves from misery, lack and limitation.

Consciousness of Spiritual Strength

When you begin to understand how to use the Power of God within you, you are Samson. In Judges 16:17, Samson said to Delilah: . . . *I have been a Nazarite unto God from my mother's womb* . . . A Nazarite means that he was consecrated to God. Samson did all kinds of athletic stunts, but was finally robbed of his strength by Delilah, who had his head shaved while he slept on her knees. *And she made him sleep upon her knees . . . she caused him to shave off the seven locks of his head; and she began to afflict him, and his strength went from him* (Judges 16:19).

Hair represents spiritual power and vitality. When the vital principle is taken away or when you permit yourself to be robbed or deprived of spiritual power, your strength and faith go with it. Strength and power come to the man who trusts the Spirit and gives all his allegiance to the One Power.

Samson's two eyes represent spiritual perception, an awareness of the Light within you. . . . *If therefore thine eye be single, thy whole body shall be full of Light* (Matthew 6:22). This means that when you put God first in your life and give all power and glory to the Divine Presence within you, then your whole embodiment, i.e., your business, home, relationship with others and all your undertakings, will reflect the Light back to you. The Philistine woman is the negative, destructive emotion which robs you of vitality, energy and enthusiasm and which depletes your entire nervous system.

He Was Vexed and Grieved

Recently I counselled a man who was highly educated and who had a responsible government position, but who was very angry, sad and depressed because the girl he had been courting and to whom he had given many expensive gifts, including an expensive engagement ring, had run off and married someone else, having said nothing to him.

I explained to him that he is not responsible for

her actions but that he is responsible for his own thoughts and emotions and that his inner rage and resentment would rob him of good discernment, health and peace of mind. He subsequently discovered that she had already been married six times, each marriage ending in a divorce with excellent financial benefits for her. She might be said to have seduced him or tricked and deceived him by her wiles and flattery. Had he prayed for guidance and Divine companionship, this would not have happened to him.

I pointed out to him that it was not her acts which had disturbed him; it was his own opinions and thoughts which had done so. If he were to take away his opinions and resolve to dismiss his judgment about the acts, his anger would be gone. Her wrongful act brought no shame on him. It is not what happened to him, it was his thought about it which had generated all the anger and resentment. Actually, he was taking mental poisons, generated by himself; she had nothing to do with it.

He saw what he was doing to himself and stopped it. He released the woman in his mind, blessed her and walked on. Remember, where there is no opinion there is no suffering, and where there is no judgment there is no pain.

Seven Locks of Hair

The number seven is frequently mentioned in the Bible: the seventh day, the seventh hour, the seventh vial, etc. The word sabbath means seven; it means inner certitude, inner conviction, the silent inner knowing whereby you know that your prayer is answered. Seven is one resting on one, meaning you rest in God, your sense of atonement with your ideal. The sabbath in the Bible has nothing to do with days of the week. Six days represent the length of time it takes you to impregnate your subconscious mind. It has nothing to do with time; all it means is that it refers to the moment of the embodiment of your desire in your subconscious. This is followed by a period of mental and spiritual pregnancy; then comes the manifestation as the joy of the answered prayer.

The number seven is dramatized in nature also, as depicted in the solar spectrum. Pass a beam of sunlight through the beveled edge of a piece of glass and it is broken up into seven colors. The diatonic scale consists of seven different tones.

Cutting off the seven locks of hair is depriving you of your oneness with God and your faith and confidence in the Only Power there is. Symbolically, this woman cut off this man's seven locks of hair because he permitted himself to get angry and agitated and emotionally distraught, thereby robbing and stealing from himself peace, harmony, wholeness and vitality. If a cucumber is bitter, don't eat it; throw it away. If you find briars on the road, turn aside from them. Suppose you heard that another man had been lying about you and saying all manner of evil about you;

his sayings have no power to prevent your mind from remaining pure, wise, sober and just.

Consider Your Opinion

Marcus Aurelius, the great stoic philosopher, wrote *The Meditation,* which pictures with faithfulness the mind and character of one of the most noble of the Roman Emperors. Simple in style and sincere in tone, his writings record for all time the heights reached by spiritual aspiration in his effort to solve the problems of human relations. The following are quotations from his *Meditation:*

> "Consider that everything is opinion, and opinion is in thy power. Take away then when thou choosest, thy opinion, and like a mariner, who has doubled the promontory, thou wilt find calm, everything stable, and a waveless bay."
>
> "Cast away thy opinion: thou art saved. Who then hinders thee from casting it away?"
>
> "Be like a promontory against which the waves continually break, but it stands firm and tames the fury of the water around it."

These quotations reveal to you that when you have no opinion you have no suffering. If someone commits a heinous crime, it is of no use to you to get incensed and furious about it and generate destructive emotions within yourself which can ruin your health, happiness and peace of mind. It was not the incident that disturbed you; it was your thought about it.

Conquering the Lion

Samson killed a lion and found honey in the carcass. Symbolically, the lion represents any dire disaster such as an acute sickness, a so-called insoluble problem, a mountainous debt. You are told the story of Daniel in the lion's den. While locked in the den he turned his back upon the beasts and looked to God for freedom. . . . *Thy God whom thou servest continually, he will deliver thee* (Daniel 6:16).

Likewise, turn your back upon the problem and focus your attention on the solution, knowing that an Almighty Power will respond, and the prison of fear, sickness or impoverishment will disappear as you claim and know that God will reveal the answer, the solution, the way out. Acceptance of your desire is like dropping a fertile seed in the prepared soil. Turn over your desire to your subconscious as a seed, be full of confidence that it will appear in its full-blown potential, and according to your complete mental acceptance, it shall come to pass.

It is true that lions were kept in a pit and used for political punishment in those ancient days, but every story in the Bible deals with each one of us. The story of Daniel is the story of every man. Daniel, according to the Bible, made a habit of prayer, praying regularly many times a day. This practice prepared him and enabled him to overcome. Samson found honey in the carcass of the lion he slew. Likewise, you get great satisfaction and joy in overcoming your problem by prayer.

The Real Causes

The real causes of all our problems lie within ourselves. The enemies we overcome are fear, doubt, self-condemnation, ignorance and so forth. *And a man's foes shall be they of his own household* (Matthew 10:36).

Recently I talked with a teacher who had remained in a subordinate position for four years because she was under the impression that her qualifications were not sufficient to advance to a higher position in the college. I suggested that she inquire further and discuss the matter with one of the senior professors. She did so and found that there was no such restrictive regulation. She then applied for a new assignment and was accepted with a big increase in salary. This had been a false belief in her own mind; it had no reality but was created by herself. She could have overcome the situation at any moment.

All of us should cease believing in helpless submission to all kinds of supposed lack and limitation. For example, many people believe they are too old to do something that they are really quite capable of doing. Professional hunters tell us that no wild animal in the jungle will attack a man who is not afraid of it. Animals scent fear and will attack. In India it is well known that many outstanding true Yogis can walk and live among tigers, lions, snakes and other beasts of prey in perfect safety. They are at that level of consciousness where they see the Presence of God in all creatures. They build up an immunity through the practice of the Presence of God and become God-intoxicated, receiving the Divine antibody, which is a true realization in the heart that everything you see is Spirit, or God, in manifestation. They translate everything back to God, or Spirit, and one part of Spirit cannot be antagonistic to another part of Spirit. This is a sense of oneness with all life.

How She Trampled on the Lion

Some months ago I had a telephone call from a woman in Pasadena, who told me that she was considered a terminal case. She had much to live for, however, having two young boys to bring up and care for, as they had no father. The father had passed on to the next dimension.

I explained to her that her intense desire to live and her love for the two boys was wonderful spiritual medicine. She cooperated with her doctor, blessing him and the medication which alleviated the pain to a great extent. She had an excellent knowledge of the laws of mind and of spiritual healing techniques. She began to affirm feelingly and knowingly: "I am alive with the Life of God and I give thanks for the miraculous healing taking place now."

She has had three X-rays recently, all of which were negative. Her intense desire to live was a tremendous stimulus to her recovery. Her habitual thinking had found its way by spiritual osmosis to her subconscious mind and a healing followed.

Do Others Disturb You?

Marcus Aurelius says: "Art thou angry with him whose arm-pits stink? Art thou angry with him whose mouth smells foul? What good will this anger do thee? He has such a mouth, he has such arm-pits: it is necessary that such an emanation must come from such things—but the man has reason, it will be said, and he is able, if he takes pains, to discover wherein he offends—I wish thee well of thy discovery. Well then, and thou hast reason: by thy rational faculty stir up his rational faculty; show him his error. For if he listens, thou wilt cure him, and there is no need of anger."

Likewise, you may see a hunchback or a cripple. You are not angry or upset; in all probability you would have compassion for his deformity and wish for him all the blessings of life. Sometimes when walking through the woods or climbing a mountain, you may see some pine trees which usually grow straight and heavenward. It is said the ancient called the tree a pine tree to remind him that they were pining or hungering after God. However, you may come across some pine trees that are twisted, crooked and deformed. This condition may be due to some early influence when the tree was a sapling—a fence, a stone or a ditch may have interfered with its normal growth. You do not see the original cause, but you see the effect of the early influence.

Likewise, when you meet a person with a sour, nasty and ugly disposition, undoubtedly he was mal-conditioned and abused mentally when young. All children are naturally loving; they crave and give love freely. You understand why he is the way he is and you refuse to be upset by his sour disposition. Obviously, he is deformed mentally, but he is in a position to recondition his mind whenever he decides to do so. Your understanding causes you to abstain from criticism, resentment or hatred because of his warped mentality.

The Only Way

You will often come across people who will inform you that they have a corner on Truth and that their religious faith or belief is the "only way." Our Bible is full of legends, parables, and myths which teach the truth about God, Life and the Universe. You can't put anything into a closed mind any more than you can add any more to a full cup. You are in the presence of Infinity and never in eternity could you exhaust all the wonders and glories of Infinity. There is no end to our growth in wisdom, truth and beauty.

There is an old legend which conveys a profound truth. It is said that in ancient times when the world was young there was a conclave of the gods held on Mount Olympus. The purpose of this august meeting was to decide whether men and women on this earth plane should be entrusted with the Truth so that they could fashion their lives after the gods. After a long debate, pro and con, the elder gods came to the conclusion that they would give the greatest treasure of all to man—the "Jewel of Truth."

It is said that one of the junior gods had long been pleading with the elder gods for some outstanding mission to perform for the benefit of humanity, regardless of its danger or difficulties. His motive was to win the approbation of the elder gods. He was finally granted permission to descend to earth and give the "Jewel of Truth" to all men here below. He was ecstatic about his new adventure and was bubbling over with enthusiasm and somewhat overwhelmed by the wonders of it all—that he alone was the chosen one to bring the Truth to man.

The legend says that just as he made a landing on earth, he unfortunately stumbled and fell, and the "Jewel of Truth," which was dashed to the ground, was scattered into thousands and thousands of particles all over the good earth! The gods on Mount

Olympus were disturbed and upset, and the young god was very repentent and depressed over it. The reason for his sorrow was that his accident caused no end of trouble and confusion, because forever after, men found *particles* of the jewel and each man fancied that *he alone* had found the *Truth*.

There is only One Truth, One God, One Law, One Life. God is the Truth, and the Truth is the same yesterday, today and forever. No one has a monopoly on the Truth. God is the way, the truth and the life. The Bible says . . . *I am the way, the truth, and the life* . . . (John 14:6). I AM means Being, Life, Awareness, or God. The laws of mind are the same for everybody throughout the world; so are the laws or principles of chemistry, physics, mathematics or astronomy. The laws of agriculture, like the laws of navigation, work for all men alike. A good basic book to read on the laws of mind is *The Power of Your Subconscious Mind.**

The above legend is the answer to all those who have the "only way," a "special revelation" or the "one true way."

He Failed in Business

In consultation with a young man who had developed arthritis, which was very painful (even the drugs he was taking did not always relieve the acute pain),

**The Power of Your Subconsious Mind* by Dr. Joseph Murphy, Prentice-Hall, Inc., Englewood Cliffs, N.J., 1963.

it was revealed that his father had installed him in business and had advanced him a large sum of money. Although he worked very hard, he had failed and had gone into bankruptcy. He feared his father's rebuke and scorn, however. He was "down on himself" and full of self-condemnation. Soon after his failure, he developed arthritis. This was the emotional cause behind his physical impairment.

I pointed out to him that his repressed emotions had to find an outlet somewhere, and that the internal pressure must find some organ through which it can explode. The result—an illness or inflammation which is physical in expression but emotional in origin. This man was not the business type but went into business to please his father. He had previously been a teacher in high school and a very good one. There was no reason for self-condemnation or disgrace because he had failed.

I pointed out to him the case of a young woman who had failed as a secretary and was fired from her job, but she later turned out to be a marvelous nurse and is now head of a training unit in a hospital. She found her true place. She had not failed in life.

I suggested to him that because of his background and special training and his blend of inherited characteristics he could excel in another field of endeavor. So he went back to teaching and is now very happy about it. He talked things over with his father, admitting to him that his heart was not really in the business and that he had gone into the operation because he wanted to please him. This was followed by the removal of a sense of shame and self-criticism. They had a mutual understanding, and as soon as he took up teaching again his arthritis subsided. His new mental state was reflected in his body.

The following two prayers were the ones I suggested that he use in order to impregnate his subconscious mind and eradicate the negative patterns lodged there. The first was the prayer of forgiveness, which is self-explanatory and is as follows:

Prayer for Forgiveness

"I claim God's love fills my soul now. I know when His love flows in my heart, as all resentment is dissolved. I forgive myself for harboring any negative, destructive thoughts about another. I resolve not to do this any more. I tune in on the Infinite One within me, and I think, speak, act and react from the standpoint of God and His law of love. I fully and freely forgive everyone (mention their names). I radiate love, peace, goodwill and all the blessings of Heaven to them. They are free and I am free. I know when I have released others because I can meet them in my mind and there is absolutely no 'sting'; on the contrary, there is a wave of peace and a benediction from my heart."

The Law of Progress

The second prayer, which was to be used three times out loud every morning, is as follows:

"I am a mighty tower of strength and stability in the realization that God is my unfailing Source. I give freely, willingly, lovingly of the talents I have. I serve loyally and efficiently, knowing that my service is recognized and compensated.

"My consciousness is ever expanding into larger fields of activity. I increase, daily, my mental measure of success. I attune myself to success in every way. I am alert to new ideas that lead to successful activity.

"Richness of faith and increased activity bring me rich results, for the Power within me knows no limitation. My salary is a measure of my spiritual values. My faith and expectancy create my income. My wealth is based on Universal Substance and my measure of acceptance determines the amount of compensation. I accept all good that is ever flowing to me, now."

CHAPTER 12

Why the Passover and the Crucifixion Are Identical

The origins of the Passover and the Crucifixion are of an astronomical nature, since they are basically solar allegories. The sun in the order of nature crosses the equator twice every year, and you will find in the New Testament allegory that there are actually two Crucifixions, and Christ (the Sun) is said to be crucified twice—that is, once upon Mount Calvary, *the place of the skull* (Aries) (we must use our skull or brain to find out the meaning of the allegory), and once in Egypt . . . *where also our Lord was crucified* (Revelation 11:8).

The vernal crucifixion, or crossing of the equator by the sun, takes place on the 21st of March as our sun enters the sign of Aries. The fast of Good Friday and the feast of Easter have been religiously observed in the spring of the year in every country of the world and in every era of time of which a record of any sort has descended to us, and observed with the same ceremonies, significancy, and words.

PASSOVER AND CRUCIFIXION IDENTICAL

Christ, or Krishna, is a Hindu word meaning the Sun, which symbolically represents the Presence of God or the Eternal Light within man. The word crucifixion means to cross over; it has the same meaning as to pass over. After the pass-over, the sun ascends the heavens, but the Sun, or Christ, of the autumnal pass-over descends into hell (the winter months, below the equator).

Approximately 400 years before the birth of Jesus (who was born like all other men and who was tempted like all of us), the vernal equinoctial point—that is, the point at which the sun exactly crosses or passes over the equator—was in the first degree of the Lamb, and since that time all nations of the earth have celebrated this annual phenomenon under the allegorical veil of a crucified lamb. The sole difference between the Jewish and the Christian ceremonies is no more than that between the words *cross over* and *pass over*. This cross-over, or crucifixion, is universally celebrated at that season when the sun passes over, when it enters the constellation of the Lamb, which the Jews call the Paschal, or Passover Lamb.

In ancient times, while the sun was in the sign Pisces (sign of the fish) prior to entering Aries, people in the northern latitudes ate fish, and when the sun entered Aries, they called it "the Lamb of God that taketh away the sins of the world." This means that the sun's rays begin to melt all the ice and snow, all the seeds frozen in the earth are resurrected, and the desert rejoices and blossoms as the rose. The sun was called a savior, as it redeems us from cold, frost, hunger, and starvation. The ancients ate the flesh of the lamb in the spring in order to celebrate the vernal equinox, and they drank the blood in honor of the autumnal crucifixion—the blood being nothing other than the blood of the grapes, which are ripe in September.

The great research scholar, Robert Taylor of St. John's College, Cambridge, England, in his *Astronomico-Theological Discourses,* delved into ancient archives in his research work and stated that in the year 680, under the reign of Constantius Pogonatus, in the Sixth Constantinopolitan Council, held under Pope Agathus, in the 82nd Degree of that Council, it was decreed (and the decree subsequently ratified by Pope Adrian the First) that instead of Christ being represented under the form of a crucified lamb, which had up to that time been the only emblem of the crucifixion, he should be represented in the hideous and disgusting form of a crucified man. Taylor also said, "I have the happiness of showing you on the unquestionable authority of the pious Casalius, a plate of the oldest form of the crucifix, preserved in the Vatican, where you see Christ is represented as a bleeding lamb, standing upon a mount under the cross, and bleeding from his five wounds, one in each foot, and the fifth from the breast, in allegory of the five winter months, Oct., Nov., Dec.,

Jan., Feb., during which the sun really and literally is, below the cross, precisely as in the sacred Hieroglyph you see him represented."

The five wounds are our five senses which are governed by appearances and are therefore "below the horizon." When we spiritualize our five senses, we will resurrect the Light or Intelligence of God, which symbolizes the resurrection of the sun in Aries.

The Jewish Passover is described in Exodus 12:3-10: *. . . They shall take to them every man a lamb . . . without blemish . . . And they shall take of the blood, and strike it on the two side posts and on the upper door post of the houses, wherein they shall eat it . . . roast it with fire . . . and ye shall let nothing of it remain until the morning; and that which remaineth of it . . . ye shall burn with fire.*

The Passover means the joy in awakening from darkness to light; it means the delivery from misery and pain to the truths that make man free. It means passing from one state of mind to another. The lamb is chosen as it is a world symbol of sacrifice: it is born in order to die for human advantage. The lamb gives man wool, clothing, and meat. The symbol for lamb in Chinese is composed of sheep and fire; that is, it pictures a sheep on the fire, as though the peculiar appropriation and destiny of lambs were for sacrificial offerings. Confucius stated that a lamb constituted an ancient sacrifice of great importance. The lamb is your desire. All that is necessary is to feel its reality, and to live, move, and act as though it were a fact *now*. Your belief will bring it to pass. The only thing you give to God is recognition and faith in Him.

Ye shall eat nothing leavened. . . . Draw out and take you a lamb according to your families, and kill the passover (Exodus 12:20-21). You draw out your desire from the depths of yourself. The word lamb, as previously mentioned, means your desire, idea, plan, ambition, your goal in life. Contemplate the reality of your desire. Realize that God gave you the desire and will reveal the way for its unfoldment. Pour life, love, and meaning into your desire. Animate it with feeling and enthusiasm! In other words, you have to "kill" your desire, because as long as you have the desire for health, marriage, prosperity, or a solution to your legal problem, you are frustrated and are in a divided state of mind. You must spill the life-blood of your desire, which means that as you exalt it in your mind, rejoice in its reality, and feel the joy of the answered prayer within you, it will sink into your subconscious mind and, as a seed deposited in the ground dies, so will your desire be subjectified and die and then be resurrected as the answered prayer.

You "roast" your desire (lamb) with fire, meaning that you appropriate it in consciousness completely with the fire of Divine love, leaving no room for doubt. Then you cease to desire, as the fulfillment of your wish takes place.

When you give your attention, devotion, and love to your desire, you change its nature, and, in the same way as an apple becomes a part of your blood stream, so will your desire for advancement, growth, and expansion become a living part of you. When your desire, idea, plan, or aspiration becomes a conviction, you will have "killed" the desire—that is "spilling the blood," because blood means life and you will have given your idea life and love. As you remain faithful to your ideal, you will mentally and emotionally unite with it, and your subconscious assumption or conviction will compel you to express your good in the same way that negative beliefs formerly forced you into lack and limitation.

The Bible is a spiritual book, dealing with solar allegories, parables, and analogies of all kinds. . . . *Seven days shall there be no leaven found in your houses* . . . (Exodus 12:19). This is a symbol of purification through love and forgiveness. "There must be no leaven in the house," which means that you must eradicate all ill will, hostility, bitterness, self-condemnation, and other destructive emotions in order to make room for the influx of the Holy Spirit into your heart. The Healing Presence of God does not flow through a contaminated consciousness. You must be a good conductor, and the wires which unite you with God's love, peace, and harmony are the thoughts of peace, love, goodwill, and harmony.

When your thoughts are God's thoughts, God's power is with your thoughts of good. If you are fighting or resenting your job or another person, and if you grow angry and emotionally exercised over it, that is "leaven." It is a psychic pus.

Cease giving the problem your attention! Turn to the solution, the way out! Identify with your ideals and become emotionally aroused over them, and you will ascend to the level of your ideals just as quickly as you descend to the level of your fears.

All the characters of the Bible (many of whom were historical, others fictional), live within you and represent states of consciousness, moods, tones, vibrations, and sensations. Men pray to a Jesus or to a Buddha in space, and if they believe that Jesus or Buddha or Mahomet will save them, and if they have the blind faith necessary, their prayer is answered—but they don't know how; they don't know it was their own subconscious mind that answered them.

Good Friday comes from "Fria," which means love, and love is atonement with your desire. Good Friday must be on a Friday—the day of the full moon—which means you have impregnated your subconscious fully with your desire. This is all symbolic. The moon is the reflected light of the sun. Your *sun* is your illumined conscious mind, and your subconscious always faithfully reflects your impressions on the screen of space as conditions, events and circumstances. When you are filled full of the feeling of being what you long to be, that is your *Good Friday*. The moon, in symbolic language, is your subconscious mind.

Easter, Good Friday, and Passover are not fixed dates, as are anniversaries such as the birthdays of Washington and Lincoln. The moon in its transit around the earth will come in direct opposition to the sun sometime between the 21st of March and the 25th of April. When this opposition is reached, it is called a "full moon." The first Sunday following this event is Easter Sunday; the Friday preceding Easter Sunday is observed as Good Friday.

This proves to anyone who wants to think at all that this celestial, allegorical drama has nothing to do with any man who has ever lived at any time or place; on the contrary, it has been celebrated for countless centuries to mark the ascent of the sun in its northern travels. The ancient Hebrews said that the sun shed its blood (light, life, heat) on the Passover, meaning that the actinic rays of the sun give life to all creation.

If these dates were historical, they would be the same day every year. You understand that these allegories and parables of the Bible are psychological, spiritual dramas which take place within yourself.

The sun crosses the equator, which is an imaginary line; it is a time of beginnings. When you are bubbling over with a new idea, your consciousness is ready to cross over from the old state to the new. You cross your own "equator," which is your disciplined imagination; you have the power to image or to perceive and feel that which you want; then your mind will cross over from darkness to light, from poverty to wealth, from ignorance to wisdom, from ill will to goodwill, and from fear to faith in God and in all things good. As you pour your life into your ideal, you will make it real, and you will actualize it.

Death and birth represent a constant mental and spiritual process. I must die to what I am before I can live to what I long to be. As I study the truth of the Bible, I die to superstition, and I am born to illumination and understanding. . . . *Ye shall eat it in haste: it is the Lord's passover* (Exodus 12:11). Absorb these truths quickly, joyously, and lovingly, and move forward with faith and confidence. You will become the new man in God, the happy man, the joyous man, the prosperous man, the man that God intended you to be—the inspired and Godlike man who walks the earth with the praise of God forever on his lips.

The mystical and psychological crucifixion, or passover, is to become identified with the highest ideal (the lamb without blemish), your loftiest vision, and to remain faithful to that ideal, and as you remain faithful and constant, you will crucify your desire (it crosses over from your conscious to your subconscious mind) by your faithfulness, and you will resurrect it unaided by man.

Jesus means "God saves," "God is your emancipator." It also means your desire, which, when realized, would save you from any predicament. *Judas* means your limitation or problem. Your problem reveals your savior or solution. The realization of your desire is your savior.

You are in the garden of Gethsemane when your mind is in tune with the Infinite—when your attention is focussed and absorbed on the God-Presence and when you are contemplating your ideal to the exclusion of everything else. The suicide of Judas is simply the death of limitation and the resurrection of freedom and peace of mind.

An alcoholic friend of mine dramatized the role of Jesus and Judas in this way. He wanted freedom and peace of mind (symbolized by Jesus). He began to assume freedom and peace of mind, and he imagined himself at home again with his wife congratulating him. He would sit down quietly for ten or fifteen minutes at a time and become detached from the world around about him; he focussed his mind on freedom and sobriety. He would "hear" his wife say over and over again, "Thank God, you are free—you are healed! I am so happy!" All the power of the Godhead responded to him, and he was healed.

He had completely died to his former state, and he had begun to live the new life. It was as if he had committed suicide by his own hand. He "took" his former life by becoming detached in consciousness from his former drunken state with the shakes and jitters, and he found his savior (Jesus)—the answer to his prayer, the realization of his heart's desire. Judas died and Jesus (his desire) was resurrected and made manifest.

Walk as though you now are what you want to be; sustain the mood or feeling, and you will die to the old state and resurrect the new.

The Passover or Crucifixion takes place in your own mind. There is an inner meaning to all the stories in the Bible. There must be a psychological and spiritual change in you, otherwise there is no passover. It is not only for Jews or Christians, but for all people everywhere. *Pharaoh* is the race mind moving in all of us. If you are full of fear, hatred, or resentment, or are engaging in emotional blackmail, are dominating others or are holding them in mental bondage, you are Pharaoh, and you must free yourself at once. Any corrosive, destructive thought robs you of vitality and energy and holds you in bondage.

Maintain an attitude of prayer and neutralize the corrosive, debilitating, and destructive force of the mass mind, which is full of all sorts of negative tendencies which impinge on all of us according to our degree of receptivity.

Establish one strong conviction, and that is that God is all there is. One Presence and One Power. You are one with God, and God's Spirit is sovereign, regnant, and supreme. Your belief in your oneness with God will annihilate and neutralize the false beliefs of the mass mind. You are oscillating at a higher spiritual frequency, and no evil shall befall you and no plague shall come nigh thy dwelling.

The word *nail* in the Bible means love or feeling. A young musician in my organization began to claim, feel, and picture himself as a great teacher of the science of mind. He said to me, "If two shall agree as touching on anything on earth it shall be established." He knew that the two agreeing were himself and his desire, his idea and feeling, the agreement of his conscious and subconscious mind. He affirmed for about ten minutes daily: "I am now a wonderful teacher. I am fixed in this belief. I accept it and I rejoice within. I feel, claim, and know that it is so now." He made it a point not to subsequently deny what he had affirmed.

After a few weeks, all doors opened up for him. Money, friends, opportunities, and all things needed came his way. He had "nailed himself to the cross," meaning he was nailed or fixed in his belief that his prayer was answered, and his desire crossed over to his subconscious mind; the latter compelled him to be what he felt himself to be. The law of the subconscious is compulsion.

The perpendicular beam is your I AM, or Awareness of Being, or God. The transverse beam is your belief or conviction about yourself. This is the spiritual meaning of the cross. Your own I AMness or consciousness resurrects and makes alive that which you feel as true. The cross is your conviction about God, and whatever you believe or feel to be true about God is true of yourself.

The Bible says: . . . *The Lord will pass through to smite the Egyptians; and when he seeth the blood upon the lintel, and on the two side posts, the Lord will pass over the door, and will not suffer the destroyer to come in unto your houses to smite you* (Exodus 12:23). When you have complete faith in God and are convinced that there is no other power and that God is all love, and when you have completely absorbed the reality of your desire in consciousness, you are free from all fear and doubt. Then the Lord, or Spiritual Power, will pass over the houses of Israel, and when He sees the blood—which means your living, abiding faith in God and His Truth—this conviction of yours (the angel) will pass over and kill, neutralize, obliterate, and expunge from your subconscious mind all negative patterns, be they what they may.

The firstborn of Egypt (misery, suffering, darkness, ignorance, and all negations) are destroyed, and the Light of God penetrates all the dark places of your mind. The firstborn of Egypt are the negative thoughts of the mass mind; the children of Israel means God-like thoughts, eternal verities, and the truth of God alive in your mind and heart. You are an Israelite when you feel your oneness with God, and your loyalty is to God only and . . . *If God be for you, who can be against you?* (Romans 8:31).

Live with God, walk and talk with Him, and die to human opinions. Resurrect love, life, truth, and beauty, and become the God-man here and now! This is the real Passover and the real Crucifixion.

CHAPTER 13

Change Eternal Is at the Root of All Things

There is one great Truth: God is God, the same yesterday, today and forever. Everything else is subject to change. A woman said to me recently that she was absolutely certain that she would see the president of a company who had promised her a contract over the phone. When she arrived in Los Angeles, he had passed on in his sleep. I explained to her that she could not be absolutely certain about anything in this world except that God is God, and His laws and principles never change. She turned within and affirmed knowingly that Infinite Intelligence would reveal the perfect plan for the unfoldment of her idea, and another door eventually opened up in Divine order.

He Was Certain It Was the End

While talking with a man a few months ago, he revealed that he had a cancerous condition which was incurable, and he was certain that he had only six months or less to live. I told him that there was no absolute certainty that he would not be healed. He was a student of "I Ching," and I suggested that he ask the question: "Will I be healed?" The answer he got was: "Your condition presages sickness but not death." Immediately he changed his mental attitude. Before he was certain about things that actually are not certain. He is now praying regularly and cooperating with his wholistic doctor and is on the road to victory.

There are many people who are certain that they are going to be sick or have an accident. Others make up their mind beforehand that they are not going to like another person. Many others say openly that all politicians are crooked, that all religions are rackets. Too many people form fixed ideas and dogmatic opinions about conditions, circumstances and people, which are constantly changing. Remember that nothing is fixed. Nature is constantly changing; and men and women, customs, and traditions are constantly changing. Look at the works and processes of nature: Winter is summer sleeping; seasons constantly change according to a Divine pattern. The storm comes, but after that comes the calm. A flood may come but it passes away; the water abates and there comes a great peace over the area. Night comes, but it is followed by sunshine; the day breaks and all the shadows flee away.

She Said He Will Always Be a Drunkard

A mother said to me that her son is an alcoholic and will always be one. I explained to her that she should not make statements such as that, since he was subject to change like anybody else and very possibly could become a new man.

Accordingly, I gave her an age-old prayer to use night and morning: "My son John knows the Truth, he loves the Truth, he rejoices in the Truth, and he hears the Truth." It is true that everyone wants to know the Truth whether he says so or not. Shortly after her prayers had begun he went to hear Dr. William Hornaday of the Religious Science Church in Los Angeles and became a new man. Now peace and sobriety govern his mind.

The judgment of the mother was self-judgment. Cease judging the other, for the alcoholic today may be a transformed man tomorrow. The Divine Presence indwells all people and is not subject to outer and temporal considerations. Remember an age-old Hebrew maxim: "Change eternal is at the root of all things." Nothing is forever, everything changes.

He Hated His Brother

In counseling a man who had internal troubles, and who constantly took medications such as tranquilizers and sedatives, he told me that ten years previously he had been in love with a girl but that his brother had persuaded her to marry him, instead. This man had deposited the emotion of hate in the deeper recesses of his mind and nourished it every once in a while. For ten years he had refused to hold that destructive emotion of hate up to the light of reason and common sense and have it dissolved in the light of God's love.

I explained to him that he was poisoning himself and living with the dead past, somewhat like the individual who keeps the corpse of a dead person in a special room in the house and preserves it with alcohol. This, of course, is a form of insanity, as there is no one in the dead body. All of this is due probably to a sense of guilt or morbid grief, which is the opposite of love. This man was living with the dead.

He decided to forgive and forget, realizing that holding on to that old grudge or trauma was robbing him of energy, vitality, enthusiasm and health. He was building a cemetery in his own mind where all his ideals, goals and aspirations were buried in resentment, hate and ill will. His prayer was as follows: "I forgive myself for harboring these negative and destructive thoughts, and I resolve not to do this any more. I mean this, I am sincere and I decree it. I fully and freely forgive my brother and I wish for him and his wife all the blessings of life. Any time my brother comes to my mind, I will immediately affirm: 'I have released you. God be with you.' "

He kept this up, and after about ten days he said, "I can think of my brother now and there is no sting there any more," which indicated that he had expunged and eradicated the poison pocket in his subconscious mind. His health is improving now and his need for sedatives is gradually diminishing. The day will soon break for him and all the shadows in his life will flee away.

When we are sick, we have wandered away in thought from God, but we can always turn back to the One, the Beautiful, the Good, and be healed.

He Said, "What Do You Mean Saying 'God Is Principle'?"

A man asked me after a recent lecture: "What does 'God is Principle' mean?" Let us look at a few generally accepted principles with which every high school boy is familiar. "Water seeks its own level." This applies to water in any part of the world, whether China or America. It is not a particular thing or a particular action. It is a principle. Another easily understood principle is: "Matter expands when heated." This principle is true anywhere in the world, at any time, and under any and all circumstances. Heat a bar of iron anywhere and it will expand, no matter what country it is in, who possesses it, and regardless of the purpose for which it is intended.

This man had a protracted lawsuit over a will. His sister was suing him, trying to break up the will because the entire estate of his father was bequeathed to him. His sister, apparently, was very wealthy though and did not need the money. Obviously, greed was her motivation. Greed always results in lack, limitation and misery.

The first thing he had to do was to refuse to give any power to his sister, and under no circumstances resent her. He had to remain neutral and calm, realizing that God is the Principle of perfect harmony. God does not change, so perfect harmony is the nature of creation. I explained to him that prayer is answered because God is Principle and that he has to bring himself into harmony with the Law of Being. In prayer we do not try to change the Law, or God. God plays no favorites and is no respecter of persons.

He prayed as follows: "The Infinite Law of justice, truth, love and harmony operates perfectly for me and all concerned. God is the Principle of harmony, and there is a Divine solution." He kept reiterating these truths, and in a few weeks his sister withdrew from the case. Her sense of vindictiveness and greed apparently melted away under his realization of the Divine Principle of harmony operating for all concerned.

The Indwelling God

God indwells you. *God is a Spirit. . . .* (John 4:24). This Spirit is boundless love, absolute harmony, eternal, omnipotent and omniscient, and cannot be hurt, wounded or destroyed. This Spirit never changes and is the very life of you. You contact this Divine Presence through the medium of your thought. The Bible says: . . . *As he thinketh in his heart, so is he. . . .* (Proverbs 23:7). This is one of the laws of mind which is certain and is continuously demonstrated in the lives of all of us.

Your subconscious assumptions, beliefs and convictions determine all your experiences and conditions on the outside. Character is destiny. It is our state of consciousness which creates the world we live in. Consciousness is the sum total of all our thoughts, beliefs, opinions, estimates and judgments, plus our emotional reactions to them along all lines. The sum total of all our thoughts and feelings forms our state of consciousness. This consciousness commands and dictates our experiences, our health, our wealth and success in all our undertakings.

Everything Is Changing

Governments are constantly changing, as are politicians. Also, religious beliefs are constantly changing, based on the findings of science, astronomers, and physicists. Remember, change is the law of growth. You have seen the alcoholic, the dope addict and the burglar completely change their mental attitudes and begin to lead honest, good and upright lives. It is God in action in every change. Growth and expansion is the law of life.

Stop and reflect for a minute that without change there can be no growth. When man ceases to grow mentally and spiritually, his life fades away out of his dimension of life. Don't be afraid of change; cease clinging to old, moth-eaten beliefs, false creeds and dogmas. Come into the light of Truth and realize that you are here for one purpose only, and that is to release more and more of the Divinity within you. God is forever seeking expression at higher levels through you. This is called the Providence of God.

Think about this simple truth and realize that if it were not for the blessing of change, men and women would still be primitives, somewhat like savages living in caves, not knowing who you are or what you are. If it were not for change in your life, you would still be a child mentally and physically. When any change comes into your life, pronounce it good and very good. Affirm, believe, know and decree: "This change is good, and it is going to turn out and bless me," and it will. See the Presence of God in the change and that will make all things new.

She Changed Her Mind About Him and Kept It Changed

A mother complained to me about her boy, saying that he was making trouble in school, refused to study, was surly and impudent to the teachers and also to herself. She spanked him several times, but it seemed to do no good.

I suggested that she pray for Divine Intelligence operating in her son. Children respond very quickly to prayers for Intelligence. She began to pray for him several times a day, realizing that Divine Intelligence is now functioning perfectly in her boy and in all phases of his life. She discovered that his school work improved in a wonderful way, and his surly manner disappeared also.

As you pray for Divine Intelligence operating perfectly through your son or daughter, you will be pleasantly surprised to find how his or her progress in his or her studies will increase, and also how they will become happier and more successful along all lines.

Peace in This Changing World

The awareness of the Creative Power within you gives you a stability and a certainty that is necessary for a peaceful mind. Everything in this external world is constantly shifting and changing. You need a permanent and perennial anchor that you can cling to, and that is that God indwells you and that God is Infinite Spirit Which is responsive to your thought. The only immaterial power you know is your thought and feeling.

Now you have discovered the secret of creation; therefore, you can mold, fashion and create your world according to your habitual thinking and imagery. Remember, Infinite Intelligence created your body from a cell and can recreate it and heal it now. Honor and exalt this Divine Presence in you. Realize this Presence is supreme and omnipotent. Anchor yourself to the I AM or God within you, realizing that Infinite Spirit is the Source of all blessings.

Religion means "to tie back to" one great truth, God, which is eternal and the rock of your faith. Religion does not mean that you tie yourself to any creed, dogma or church, but to align yourself completely to the Living Spirit Almighty within you—the One and Only Absolute Power—Which is timeless and changeless. When troubled, vexed, annoyed or depressed, quiet your mind and affirm quietly and knowingly, *"Be still, and know that I am God"* (Psalm 46:10). This Power is within you and responds to you, giving you peace in this changing world.

The Dangers of Grief

Recently I had a conference with a woman in Atlanta, Georgia, who was grief-stricken. She had had two heart attacks. She was taking anti-depressant pills, as well as heart medicine. I discovered that she was visiting the grave of her son every day and weeping over his grave, which was a highly destructive practice. It was a morbid attitude of mind. She was dwelling on the void in her life, which consisted of no love.

I told her what Darwin had said about protracted grief: "The circulation becomes languid; the face pales; the muscles become flaccid; the eyelids droop; the head hangs on the contracted chest; the lips, cheeks and lower jaw all sink downward from their own weight." This woman was dying inside, and her mental and emotional state was the cause of all her troubles. The heart is the seat of emotion, and emotions can kill or cure.

She began to realize there was no one in the grave; her boy was in the next dimension, separated from her by frequency only. Every night she prayed for him as follows: "I rejoice in your new birthday in God. I radiate love, peace and joy to you. I know you are in another dimension of life and your journey is onward, upward and Godward. God loves you. God be with you."

I explained to her that she could not think of two things at the same time. She also came to the realization that morbid thoughts were holding her son back, as there is no separation in mind. If you love someone, you free him and send loving thoughts to him or her. Protracted grief is morbid, selfish, and destructive to health and happiness.

Wholistic Medicine

Many medical doctors today are stressing the harmful effects of negative emotions. One of the foremost doctors on wholistic medicine is Dr. Frank Varese, 24953 Paseo De Valencia, Laguna Hills, California. He points out that faith in God and in inner joy increases the defense mechanism and the activity of the leukocytes, or white blood cells, in their destruction of invading microbes or virulent bacteria. He also points out to his patients and lectures to them along similar lines that prayer, or the contemplation of the truths of God, aids in the production of antibodies and antitoxins.

On the other hand, fear, anger and hate decrease the red cells and tend to destroy them. Fear inhibits the development of antibodies and antitoxins and leaves the body subject to disease. Dr. Varese, together with other doctors, silently prays for his patients.

Jesus said frequently: . . . *Thy faith hath made thee whole* . . . (Matthew 9:22), pointing out that faith in God was the healer.

How He Changed Fear to Faith

From time to time a submarine commander attends my lectures at the Saddleback Valley Plaza, Cinema II, 23682 El Toro Road, Laguna Hills, California. I had a very interesting conversation with him. He told me that he was at one time a pharmacist in New York City, working for a chain organization for fifty dollars a week. His doctor told him he was a chronic worrier, which was the cause of his high blood pressure. He said that he worried about his two boys and that he would not be able to send them to college. He worried that he could not buy a fur coat for his wife. He worried about a holdup in the pharmacy and lived in constant fear that he might be fired from the job, as business was slow. He worried about long hours, his future, and the fact that he would never own his own pharmacy. He worried that he would never have the money to buy a car.

When World War II came, he joined the Navy and was promoted rapidly. He said that he enjoyed the Navy. "Towards the end of the war," he related, "our submarine was attacked from all sides and I submerged as we were hopelessly outmanned and outgunned. The enemy ships kept dropping depth charges and we remained submerged for 20 hours. There was nothing to do but wait and pray. At any moment I and the other men could have been annihilated. Some of the men said, 'This is the end.' I said, 'God help us. The Lord is our shepherd.' "

These were the only spiritual words he could think of, and in his extremity he kept repeating these words audibly. He began to think of all the other things in his life as a pharmacist that he had worried about. He saw that all of them were trivia and of no consequence compared to what he and his men were now experiencing. He silently said to himself, "If I ever see the moon and the stars again, I'll never worry all the days of my life." And, as a matter of fact, he has not worried since and is full of faith in God and all things good.

His prayer was answered and they were not killed. All of his lesser fears had paled into insignificance compared to the terror and extreme danger of his submarine experience.

Face the Challenge and You Will Overcome

Face your fears. Look at them. Are they real? Is there any principle behind them, or are they all imaginary and created by yourself? Do these fears have a reality, or are they a conglomeration of sinister shadows created by your warped and distorted mind?

Emerson once said, "Do the thing you are afraid to do and the death of fear is certain." If you are afraid to speak before an audience, the thing to do is to get up and speak for a minute or two before any audience you can find, and after a few times, all the fear will go away. You discover that a Power comes to your aid which gives you courage, faith and confidence. When you discover the Power, fear goes away. When you speak or give a lecture, affirm: "God thinks, speaks and acts through me. It is wonderful!" God is your partner and you are equipped for all occasions.

His Dogged Persistence Did Not Pay Off

I suggested to a man that he stop fighting the Food and Drug Administration. He had gone to court after court, insisting that he was right and refusing to admit defeat. This attitude never works, because he was giving power to the FDA. He believed the odds were against him. He was beaten again and again in court, even though he refused to admit it.

Regardless of his persistence and doggedness, he was bound to fail because it is done unto him as he believes. . . . *As thou hast believed, so be it done unto thee* . . . (Matthew 8:13). No matter how courageous and persistent he was, inwardly he believed that the odds were against him; therefore, he could not win.

He discontinued his litigation at that point and gave attention to his business, which had been neglected. Things happen to us according to our belief, which is not merely an intellectual assent, but a belief that is emotionally charged and is lodged in our heart (subconscious mind). The Bible says: *For as he thinketh in his heart, so is he* . . . (Proverbs 23:7). Whatever we really feel to be true deep down in our hearts is the thing that governs, rules and leads us.

Never look upon your environment as a cause. Never give power to other people, conditions or events. Causation is within, and you do not give power to externals. Your consciousness, the way in which you think, feel and believe, and whatever you give your mental consent to will govern your life. Realize that God (the Spirit within you) is the only creative power. Accept this and you will be freed from a thousand false beliefs and the thralldoms of the world.

Peace Cannot Be Legislated

Peace comes from God, for God is Absolute Peace. Fear causes people to be angry and resentful and ugly in their relations with others. As men and women learn to let Divine love fill their minds and hearts, they will become peaceful and happy people with a feeling of goodwill to all. It is well known that a happy man is a healthy man and also a moral man. If a man is at peace with himself, he has no desire to mar or hurt the life of another person. He does not disturb the peace and happiness of the other person.

Most of man's fears are due to making the external world a cause when factually it is an effect. Sickness does not come from the outside. Disease is a lack of peace of mind. Externals are subservient to the spiritual convictions of man. Knowing that the inside governs the outside causes men to rest from their fears and anxieties. All things that happen to us are due to our inward beliefs, convictions and commitments. Knowing this, you can easily get the world off your shoulders. It is your thought about the event or circumstance that matters.

You are free to think, and you are responsible for the way in which you think. The enemies are in our own mind. Your mind is now one with God, and your thoughts are God's thoughts. God's power is with your thoughts of good. You pronounce things and events good or bad according to the way you fear or love. It is your personal relationship with events that determines the nature of your fear or love. Keep walking in the Light, for there is nothing good or bad, but thinking makes it so.

Change from Fear to Divine Love

Think about God's love. Analyze it, claim it, and begin to realize that all the love of men and women throughout the world is but a faint reflection of the Infinite ocean of love. God's love is written in your heart and inscribed in your inward parts.

A woman said to me that she had prayed for a healing for many months and there was not the slightest improvement. The world is governed by law, and there is no such thing as a broken law. When our prayers are not answered it must be because we have not fulfilled the conditions of the law. Ninety-nine times in a hundred it is because we lack a sense of love for all and the spirit of forgiveness. This woman had a deep-seated grudge against another woman who had deceived her and who had extracted a large sum of money from her under false pretenses.

Being in Truth, she realized she had attracted this experience to herself and admitted that she was so careless, negligent and gullible that she did not use common sense and investigate before she invested. The first step in healing is forgiveness. She knew how to forgive, and when she had really forgiven the woman by the simple procedure of knowing that when the thought of her came to her mind she no longer sizzled, then a healing followed.

You can never lose money unless you admit the loss in mind. Accordingly, she affirmed knowingly and wisely as follows: "I am mentally and spiritually identified with the money I gave _________ and it comes back to me multiplied and magnified in Divine order." Your subconscious always magnifies what you dwell upon. She was not to think of *how* it would come, as that is the secret of the subconscious. It came back to her in a very unusual way. She won over $10,000 in Las Vegas, which more than compensated for her previous loss. Love heals; fear, hate and self-condemnation damage and destroy. Claim frequently: "Divine love fills my soul." Let your words be sweet to the soul and bring health to the bones. See the Presence of God where the problem is and claim that Divine love saturates your whole being.

She Said He Was a Pillar of Strength

A woman said to me that her husband was financially very successful, but he dominated those around him in his business by the force of his domineering attitude and willpower. She wondered why he suddenly cracked up and, in her words, "went to pieces."

In talking with him, I found that he was full of fear of the future and of failure, even though he was prospering. Actually, he was afraid of life and of death. His external attitude was all bluff and bluster. He was covering it up by riding roughshod over his employees and associates. He was outwardly compensating for his inner sense of insecurity and inadequacy.

At my suggestion he began to read frequently the 27th Psalm, the greatest antidote to fear in the world today. His inner fear was calling upon his Inner Power waiting to respond to his call. Every morning he sat down quietly and prayed for all his associates and employees, as follows: "All my associates and employees are known in Divine mind. God is guiding them in all ways. I radiate love, peace and goodwill to them, and I wish for them all the blessings of life. All those connected with me are spiritual links in the chain of the growth, welfare and prosperity of our company. God thinks, speaks and acts through me."

This regular prayer every morning prior to work eventually changed his relationship with his associates and he became more amiable, affable and cordial. The mirror treatment every morning (an age-old truth) was practiced, which means he looked into the mirror every morning for about five minutes, affirming, "I am a son of the Living God. I am peaceful, harmonious and successful. God loves me and cares for me." The practice of these simple prayers transformed and changed his whole life and relationships with others.

Change Your Concept of Yourself

I have talked with outstanding doctors, chemists, actors and businessmen who were born in the ghettos of New York and other cities. They said to me with but slight variation that they had a dreadful sense of inferiority and inadequacy in comparing themselves to the well-dressed and well-fed boys in the local schools. They wanted to succeed and excel and had a deep urge to rise, transcend, and be somebody. Their sense of inferiority was a spur and a great incentive urging them on to victory.

One outstanding surgeon born in an area known as Hell's Kitchen in New York, said to me: "I decided to prove to myself that others had no more ability or intelligence than I had." He said that his sense of inferiority and poverty drove him to excel and put his head above the crowd. . . . *Let the weak say, I am strong* (Joel 3:10).

The following prayer is good spiritual medicine: " 'A merry heart doeth good like a medicine, but a broken Spirit drieth the bones.' I am ever joyous, active, and energetic. I am always passing on God's ideas to my fellowman and I give him peace, joy, and happiness. 'In thy presence is fullness of joy; at thy right hand there are pleasures for evermore.' 'The joy of the Lord is my strength.' I am always cheerful, free, and full of happiness. I have dominion over all things in my world; I sense and feel my oneness with God, with life, the universe, and all things. I am perfectly adjusted emotionally. I meditate on whatsoever things are lovely, good, wonderful, and God-like. The peace of God is mine now, and I stir up the gift of God which is joy. I am truly a son of the living God, and 'all the sons of God shouted for joy!' "

CHAPTER 14

How to Experience Good Fortune in Your Life

Recently a friend of mine placed a large sum of money on a horse and lost. His statement was, "Just my luck. Misfortune in investments seems to haunt me." His brother, attending the same race, won large sums of money. His attitude was, "I am always fortunate. I believe in good fortune and I expect good fortune at all times." You can see the difference in mental attitudes. Changed attitudes change everything in your life. One brother's attitude was, "Good fortune never happens to me." It is always done unto us as we believe. The law of life is the law of belief. . . . *Go thy way; and as thou hast believed, so be it done unto thee* . . . (Matthew 8:13).

A professional gambler told me that he never gambles until a certain inner mood, feeling or conviction wells up in him; then he knows he will win, and he does. When the feeling of good fortune leaves him, he immediately stops playing.

In a recent visit to San Diego, I met a man in the

Little America Westgate Hotel where I usually stay when I visit there. He told me he was from New Orleans and that he comes to Southern California every year during the racing season. He had read *The Power of Your Subconscious Mind** and used it in the following way, establishing his own technique: Every night prior to sleep he would study one outstanding race, read up on the horses' previous performances, etc., and then he would say to his subconscious mind: "You are all-wise. You know the winner. Reveal to me the answer." Then he would lull himself to sleep with one word, "Winner, winner, winner." He said that he usually sees the race run in his dream. He knows the winner and bets accordingly. He claims that he has made a fortune in that way. He says that when he fails it is always due to his fear of playing favorites in his own mind.

Know Your Real Father, Which is God

In one of our Bible classes where we teach the inner meaning of the Bible, a woman asked me to explain the meaning of the following verse from Deuteronomy: *A bastard shall not enter into the congregation of the Lord; even to his tenth generation shall he not enter into the congregation of the Lord* (Deuteronomy 23:2).

*See *The Power of Your Subconscious Mind* by Dr. Joseph Murphy, Prentice-Hall, Inc., Englewood Cliffs, N.J., 1963.

This, of course, is not to be taken literally. The Bible teaches psychology and metaphysics, the laws of life and the way of the Infinite Spirit. The Bible is full of metaphors, similes and figures of speech. A bastard does not know his father. This is the Bible's way of saying that when man does not know his Source, Which is God, he does not know his own inner potentials. Our genealogy is from God.

All religions teach that God is our Father. All of us have a Common Progenitor, and we are all intimately related. A man who knows his Source and his oneness with the Father of All experiences good fortune in his life. *Acquaint now thyself with him, and be at peace: thereby good shall come unto thee* (Job 22:21). There is always a wonderful sense of wholeness, well-being and peace when you discover you are one with the Infinite, one with First Cause.

If you think you are simply a son of John Jones and governed by your environment and immediate heredity, then your prospects, ideals and expectations are very limited and restricted. Children come through the father and mother but not by them. Your true Father is God, the Universal Life-Principle. Realizing that to be true causes you to expect nothing but good fortune and all the blessings of life. You are empowered to contact this Universal Supreme Power, enabling you to work wonders in your life. To take the Bible verse literally in Deuteronomy which the young woman asked about would be absurd and meaningless, because many so-called illegitimate sons have quite obviously reached great heights in science, the arts, industry, and in all other phases of life.

A person not knowing the Source of all good is covered by darkness and lacks vision. He is subject to all the negative propaganda of the world and the impressions, illusions and false beliefs of the mass mind, and that is what misfortune really is. He thinks he is a victim of circumstances, conditions and environment and that these determine his fortune in life. Many people with whom I talk are full of fear of old age and insecurity. They believe they are victims of fate and chance.

To experience good fortune, you go back to the realization that you are a son or daughter of the Infinite, that you are free to mold, fashion and shape your destiny irrespective of what other people say or do and regardless of conditions around you. Right thinking is the law of the day. . . . *What doth the Lord thy God require of thee, but to fear* (revere, respect) *the Lord thy God, to walk in all his ways, and to love him, and to serve the Lord thy God with all thy heart and with all thy soul?* (Deuteronomy 10:12).

You are an offspring of Divinity, and you realize externals are not causative; they are an effect, not a cause. You are a causationist and you become what you contemplate and feel to be true. Your external world is an accurate and mathematical reflection of your habitual thinking, imagery and beliefs. In other words, you literally are belief expressed. Expect good fortune, harmony, health, peace, joy, and believe in the goodness of God in the land of the living. *For the Lord is good; his mercy is everlasting; and his truth endureth to all generations* (Psalm 100:5).

He Experienced Great Good Fortune

A man living here in Leisure World in Southern California, told me that he had suffered from a chronic ailment for many years which was not healed by the usual, orthodox medical treatment. He was asked to join a pilgrimage to Lourdes, France. On bathing in the waters, there occurred a complete healing, and he was free of symptoms for many years; but then the condition returned. In the first instance he went along expecting and believing that he would be healed. This is called faith healing, which means he did not know how he was healed, but since his mind had not been changed, the old condition returned.

Faith healing is important. People are healed by placebos, by talismans, relics, bones of so-called saints, etc., or anything else that moves the mind from fear to faith. This man, however, lived in fear that the old condition would return, and, of course, it did. He got a complete healing by forgiving himself for holding an old grudge and resentment against a former partner. He got rid of the poison pocket in his subconscious mind and then had a real spiritual healing. He knew what he was doing and why he was healed. A relapse will not occur, since he completely forgave himself and the other person.

The Psychic Sea

All of us are immersed in this great psychic sea, which consists of the thinking, fears, and false beliefs of four and a half billion people. If we do not keep prayed up we may become ill or experience misfortune and loss and not know why it happened. We must learn to think right, feel right and act right.

Disease Is of the Mind

Disease is not independent of man. For example, you do not go into a pharmacy and ask for half a pound of heart disease or tuberculosis, neither do you ask for arthritis or any other ailment. Disease is a lack of peace of mind. It means a mind disturbed, based on erroneous thinking and negative, destructive emotion. . . . *I will cure them, and will reveal unto them the abundance of peace and truth* (Jeremiah 33:6).

In spiritual healing, we realize that our life is God's life, the Omnipresent Spirit, Which is God, the Principle of Wholeness. It is the Spirit of God that heals and makes us whole.

He Was Burning Inwardly

In consultation with a man, he told me that he was burning inside. Indeed, he was because his tissues were inflamed and he had what is called an acute attack of arthritis brought on by his own poisonous, corrosive thoughts, which were sending out ugly, negative vibrations. A former partner of his had doctored the books and had run off with over $200,000. He was suffering from suppressed rage, which had affected his entire being and had also brought loss and misfortune along all lines. This prolonged bitterness was like a smoldering fire emanating ugly vapors, ruining his health and finances.

I suggested to him that he sit down and think over the situation and try to determine how his partner was able to swindle him of $200,000 without his knowledge. Was it carelessness or negligence on his part or that of his accountant? Gradually he allowed the anger to pass, though, realizing the futility of the resentment and anger, which was self-induced. He saw that he had erred also in not checking the books and not observing the daily routine business procedure. He began to understand that it was necessary for him to forgive, not so much for the sake of the other as for his own sake. To forgive means to give for, to exchange the bitter, ugly emotion for a constructive emotion.

The person who refuses to forgive burns up the bridge to his health, happiness and peace of mind. His wife was French, and she told him about Victor Hugo, who was banished to an island by Napoleon.

He gazed at the ocean for a long time and then cast a pebble into the ocean. He was throwing his bitterness and hostility into the sea, where it was drowned. He rose above self-pity and resentment.

This man said, "I definitely release my ex-partner to God. God made him and created him, and I wish for him all the blessings of life. I mean this, I am sincere, and I decree it is done." I explained to him that having done it once, there was no occasion to repeat it because he meant it, and whenever the thought of his ex-partner came to his mind, he would affirm, "I have released you. God be with you."

After a week or so using this discipline, his peace of mind returned and once again good fortune smiled on him. This man realized that his former resentment had tied up a lot of energy, vitality and good judgment. He was carrying a weight in his mind which resulted in loss of health, wealth and inner peace. This man then decided to raise his sights of achievement and acccomplishment and let his energy flow along constructive channels. His vision was on wholeness—perfect health and to give better service to others. His business flourished almost immediately and gave him respect and good fortune along all lines.

The kingdom of God is within you. It is a kingdom because you are a king over your conceptive realm—over your thoughts, ideas, images, actions and reactions. In other words, the kingdom of God is the invisible world of your own thought and feeling, which permeates your entire life. You have the authority and the government is on your shoulders. Your thought and feeling control your destiny. In ancient times the king was an absolute monarch and had the power of life and death over his subjects. You are an absolute monarch over your life. You can refuse a passport to any negative thought or morbid suggestion, and you also have the power to cremate and burn up every hateful, angry thought with the fire of Divine love.

Tranquilizers Did Not Cure Her Misfortune

In consultation with a woman in Las Vegas, Nevada, she pointed out that she had lost a quarter million dollars in gambling in the casinos. Her doctor had prescribed Valium for her, a tranquilizer. She took large doses of it and felt good for awhile, but combining them with alcohol to offset the blues and depression brought severe bad effects, including a heart attack.

It stands to reason that pills of any kind will not give you peace, harmony, prosperity or the sense of well-being. The God of peace is within you, and you must find it there. . . . *My peace I give unto you: not as the world giveth, give I unto you* . . . (John 14:27). No one can give you this inner peace. Still your mind and affirm freely: "The currents of God's peace flow freely into my entire being and I am immersed in God's river of peace now."

Her doctor informed her that all her glands were out of order. Glands secrete hormones. The word hormone in Greek means harmony; therefore, her trouble was an acute emotional disturbance which affected all the glands in her body. She cooperated with her doctor, however, and affirmed the following prayer frequently, making sure she did not subsequently deny what she affirmed: "I now relax and let go. I am at peace. The peace that passeth understanding fills my mind. There is peace in my home, in my heart, and in all my affairs. I let go completely because I know there is a Power responding to me as I speak. This Power flows through me; it vitalizes every atom of my being. I radiate good will to all mankind. My thoughts are God's thoughts, and God's Power is in my thoughts of good. 'Be still, and know that I am God.' I am still and quiet now because I realize and know that the only Presence and the only Power indwells me. It flows in my behalf; I am at peace, and all is well. Peace, be still. I see the Truth; I love the Truth; I know the Truth. I know that in peace and in confidence lies my strength. His Life, Love, and Truth flow through me now, and I give thanks that 'It is done.'" She discovered that she secreted peace and harmony from nature's laboratory within herself.

Medical scientists point out that our brain secretes endorphin when we need it. This chemical has the same effect as morphine. In reality there is a pharmaceutical laboratory within each one of us. The person who says, "I never take drugs of any kind," forgets that his own body is constantly manufacturing drugs within himself.

Your thyroid gland, for example, is very important. It is situated below the pharynx of the neck. This hormone elaborates a complex iodine compound necessary for our growth and development. Decreased or increased activity causes severe metabolic malfunctions, causing goiter and other disturbances. There is an important functional relationship between your thyroid gland, the pituitary and the suprarenal gland.

The parathyroid adjacent to the thyroid gland elaborates an internal secretion which regulates the calcium in your body. Deficiency of this hormone results in acute toxemia, tetany and death. Extracts of the pituitary gland are quite complex and govern reproduction and many other functions of the body. Our pancreatic gland secretes insulin, and the adrenal gland secretes adrenalin, which acts as a heart stimulant, hemostatic, etc.

You can see the effect of negative, destructive emotions on these glands, producing all manner of disease and inner disturbances. All of us must learn to discover the miracle-working power of the Infinite Healing Presence within us. When you tune in with the Infinite and realize that God is Spirit, and Spirit is the only Creative Power there is, and your emotions and feelings represent the Spirit, you must ask yourself how you are using the Spirit within you—constructively or destructively? Diabetics are blessed because they can introduce insulin into their bodies and compensate for the deficiency within them.

Remember that God is your Creator, and all of us have the capacity to re-create ourselves. *Know ye that the Lord he is God: it is he that hath made us, and not we ourselves; we are his people, and the sheep of his pasture* (Psalm 100:3). When you pray frequently as follows, you will find all your organs functioning in Divine law and order: "God is, and His Presence flows through me as harmony, beauty, love, peace, joy, right action and strength. Serenity and tranquility reign supreme in my mind and body."

The Psalmist said, *I will lift up mine eyes unto the hills, from whence cometh my help* (Psalm 121:1). Here the Psalmist is saying that you should turn your eyes to the Divine Presence within you, which also made the stars and the galaxies of space, realizing that there is an Infinite wisdom and power governing all things—a wisdom which started our own heartbeat. As we dwell upon the beauties and the glories of the Infinite One, we, too, shall be lifted up above the petty strifes and vexations of the day.

Begin to realize that the whole world is really a thought of God. Furthermore, we begin to contemplate that the Spirit within us is God—the only Creative Power. When our thoughts are God's thoughts,

God's power is with our thoughts of good. The Guiding Principle Which guides the planets in their courses and which causes the sun to shine is within you and will respond to your thought. *He shall call upon me, and I will answer him* . . . (Psalm 91:15).

Turning in recognition to God and giving all your devotion and loyalty to the One Power is called loving God, and when you do this, the law of reciprocal relationship takes over and God's love flows through you in transcendent loveliness, healing and restoring your soul. Good fortune automatically follows when you turn for guidance and inspiration from The One, The Beautiful and The Good.

Good Fortune Follows the Focus of Your Attention

Whatever you focus on and give your attention to, your subconscious magnifies and multiplies. Focus your mental lens on Divine right action, Divine law and order, Divine beauty and Divine love. Then you will discover all these qualities of God are manifested in your life. As you continue along these lines you will be actively turning your eyes to the hills from whence cometh your help.

Thou wilt keep him in perfect peace, whose mind is stayed on thee . . . (Isaiah 26:3). *I will both lay me down in peace, and sleep: for thou, Lord, only makest me dwell in safety* (Psalm 4:8). Remember, it is not pills or capsules or other people that give you peace and tranquility, but, rather, your contemplation of the truths of God from the highest standpoint. You become what you contemplate, and as you contemplate the eternal verities, you will find rest in mind and body. Peace of mind and good fortune will follow you all the days of your life.

The Years Teach Much that the Days Never Tell

The great truths of life are eternal—the same yesterday, today and forever. Whenever we think we have discovered a new truth, we find that it was always known. We have had the Golden Rule for thousands of years, and if people followed it, there would be no strife, war, crime, or inharmonious human relations; we would experience heaven on earth. All religions teach it and have done so as far back as we can go in history.

. . . *When thou prayest, enter into thy closet, and when thou hast shut thy door, pray to thy Father which is in secret; and thy Father which seeth in secret shall reward thee openly* (Matthew 6:6). The purpose of all prayer is to contact and experience the Presence of God. Whatever good we pray for, be it health, peace, harmony, guidance, or love, already subsists in the Divine Presence within us. The Father within is the Source of our life and the Progenitor of all things visible and invisible. Our thought and feeling is the Father or Source of all things.

She Was Trying to Convert Everybody in the Office

A young woman was fired from her position because the manager said she was a religious nut and was trying to convert everyone in the office by giving them pamphlets and telling them what she had learned about the mind and the inner meaning of the Bible. This young woman had listened to six or seven lectures in Truth and became healed of an oppressing difficulty. She was so happy about it that she wanted to pour out her discovery to others indiscriminately.

I explained to her that this procedure is usually very unwise. The Bible says: *Give not that which is holy unto the dogs, neither cast ye your pearls before swine, lest they trample them under their feet, and turn again and rend you* (Matthew 7:6). Many to whom she had talked had fixed religious beliefs and they resented her intrusion. Her associates in the office were not ready for a change, and when people's minds are not open and receptive to the Truth, no amount of persuasion or discussion will make them so. When in doubt, the best thing to do is to pray for guidance, and the Infinite Spirit will reveal to you whether you should introduce the subject of Truth or not. Remember, if you make it a habit to pray regularly for wisdom, Divine guidance and a desire to serve people, the law of attraction will work for you and at the right time the right people will be drawn to you.

This young woman foolishly tried to convert her father, mother and brothers to her way of thinking. They resented her approach very much and accused her of being brainwashed by some weird cultists. She realizes now that all she got for her pains in her home was a lot of friction, discord and ill feeling. The best way to spread the Truth is by living the Truth. She has learned her lesson in life and now realizes that relying on God's guidance will cause her to say the right thing at the right time—all in Divine order.

The Present Tense

Always pray in the now. For example, suppose you are studying for an examination a year from now. The right approach is to pray about it now, in the present tense. Do not wait until the time comes, but pray about it now. The fact that you are thinking about it means it is present in your mind. The thought is a present one; you deal with it at this moment.

God is outside of what we call time. The only thought you should be concerned about is the present one. The thoughts of twenty years ago do not matter; all you need do is get the present thought right and everything else will be right.

Love Thy Neighbor as Thyself

It says "as thyself," which means that the Real Self of you is God—your Higher Self—the Living Spirit Almighty called the Life-Principle. That is the reality of you. If you do not love the God-Presence within you, you really cannot love anybody. Your neighbor is the closest thing to you, "closer than breathing and nearer than hands and feet."

It is the Divine Presence within you that is your real neighbor, and to love this neighbor is to have a very healthy, reverent, wholesome respect for the Divinity Which created you and gave you the whole world. Furthermore, to love God means you give all your allegiance, loyalty and devotion to the God-Presence within, knowing It to be Primal Cause, Supreme and Omnipotent, and you positively, definitely and absolutely refuse to give power to any created thing in the world. When you honor and exalt the Divinity within yourself, you automatically respect the Divinity in others.

She Said that They Were Mean to Her

One young woman complained to me that she had had a number of different jobs, and that wherever she went, the boss and her associates were always mean to her. She was down on herself and was constantly criticizing herself and full of self-condemnation. Therefore, others treated her the same way that she was treating herself.

Being mean and nasty to herself, she could not possibly think harmoniously and lovingly of others. She was projecting her thoughts and feelings onto those around her, and they picked up her negative vibrations and acted accordingly. Having a very low estimate of herself, and being down on herself, she was projecting negative thoughts which tended to drag others down with her. She had to learn to love herself and have a healthy and wholesome respect for the Spirit Which created her.

The prayer discipline prescribed for every morning was as follows: "I am a daughter of God. God loves me and cares for me. God is my Father, and I give all honor and glory to the God-Presence within me." She practiced this prayer therapy before the mirror every morning for about five minutes and also at night prior to sleep. When she was prone to criticize, demean or demote herself during the day, she resolved to immediately supplant the negative thought with this spiritual affirmation: "I exalt God in the midst of me."

After several weeks of this spiritual discipline she ceased self-condemnation and self-criticism. Her whole life pattern has changed since she realized that she really is a daughter of the Infinite and a child of Eternity. She exudes vibrancy and goodwill to those around her, and she has found peace in this changing world.

He Despises Himself

Dr. Frank Varese, a medical doctor practicing wholistic medicine, told me that he was surprised at the number of people, both men and women, who neglect their bodies and look for the cheapest food; yet they are very wealthy and could afford the finest and best food. They wear old clothes and operate old, run-down automobiles; they neglect their bodies and forget what Paul said: "Glorify God in your body." The doctor said that they love money more than themselves. They have forgotten that they can't take it with them, and when they go on to the next dimension, usually all the relatives engage in a lawsuit over who gets what.

If a man is depressed, dejected and down on himself, it will show up in his posture, his gait, and his speech. Remember that you are a son or a daughter of the Infinite and a child of Eternity. Never in Eternity could you exhaust the wonders and glories within you, for God is Infinite; and that means that you are Infinite. To love yourself, spiritually speaking, is not mere elephantiasis of the ego, self-aggrandizement or narcissism; rather, it means to have a reverence and adoration for the Divine Presence within you, Which created you and the whole world. This is why you should exalt God in the midst of you, mighty to heal, bless and restore. Your body is also a temple of this Mystical Presence; likewise, you should treat it with respect and honor. Look upon this Divine Presence as your Heavenly Father and . . . *glorify God in your body* . . . (I Corinthians 6:20).

Use the following prayer for spiritual rebirth frequently: "Today I am reborn spiritually! I completely detach myself from the old way of thinking and I bring Divine love, light, and truth definitely into my experience. I consciously feel love for everyone I meet. Mentally I say to everyone I contact, 'I see the God in you and I know you see the God in me.' I recognize the qualities of God in everyone. I practice this morning, noon, and night; it is a living part of me.

"I am reborn spiritually now, because all day long I practice the Presence of God. No matter what I am doing—whether I am walking the street, shopping, or going about my daily business—whenever my thought wanders away from God or the good, I bring it back to the contemplation of His Holy Presence. I feel noble, dignified, and Godlike. I walk in a high mood sensing my oneness with God. His peace fills my soul."

CHAPTER 15

Faith and Confidence Lead to Victory

. . . He sendeth forth two of his disciples, and saith unto them, Go your way into the village over against you: and as soon as ye be entered into it, ye shall find a colt tied, whereon never man sat; loose him, and bring him. And if any man say unto you, Why do ye this? say ye that the Lord hath need of him; and straightway he will send him hither. And they went their way, and found the colt tied by the door without in a place where two ways met; and they loose him. . . . And they brought the colt to Jesus, and cast their garments on him; and he sat upon him. And many spread their garments in the way: and others cut down branches off the trees, and strawed them in the way. And they that went before, and they that followed, cried, saying, Hosanna; Blessed is he that cometh in the name of the Lord (Mark 11:1–4;7–9).

The colt at the crossroads is your mood, your inner feeling before entering into the deep of yourself. The crossroads represent your ability to choose, select and come to a decision. You realize that whatever you impress in your subconscious mind, whether good or bad, will be expressed on the screen of space. It is not what happens to you or what is said to you, it is your reaction to what is said or done that matters. It is your thought about it, and you have control of your thoughts. Your reactions to today's impression mold your tomorrows.

For example, if you read the newspaper and you become disgusted and angry with the news and you generate an emotional tirade of a negative nature, it enters your subconscious mind and manifests in your life. Be very careful of your reactions to events of the day, for these are the moods or tones which, when carried into the deep of yourself, come forth as form, function, experience and events.

You can stop your reaction and you can definitely control your mind. You bring your mood or feeling to Jesus, which in Biblical language means the I AM within you. Whatever you attach to I AM (Being, Life, Awareness, the Presence of God) with feeling, you will bring to pass. Take the desire of your heart, feel the reality of it, nourish it and sustain it with faith and confidence; then you are bringing the colt (the mood, the feeling) to Jesus or I AM.

Live the role, sit upon it, knowing that whatever you imagine and feel to be true will impregnate your subconscious mind and come to pass. You ride the colt (the feeling, the mood) to Jerusalem, the city of peace within yourself. Hosanna represents the joy of the answered prayer.

Blessed is he that cometh in the name of the Lord simply means the nature of the Law. The Law is that you are what you contemplate, and whatever you impress in your subconscious will be expressed. That is the law of your mind.

The Father's Business

And he said unto them, How is it that ye sought me? wist ye not that I must be about my Father's business? (Luke 2:49). Your Father's business is livingness and givingness. You are here to release and express all the qualities, attributes and potencies of God. You are placed here to lead the abundant life and express more and more of God's beauty, love and joy. Your real religion is your personal relationship with God. If you find men or women whose relationship with the Infinite makes them happy, joyous and contented, and where they get comfort from their religious beliefs, don't try to force your opinion on them.

All Things Be Ready If the Mind Be So

When man is ready, he will hear the Truth. Your mind must be open and receptive to hear the Truth, which is the same for all people of the world. It is true that prayers are answered in the orthodox church, but it is much better to know the laws of mind and use the laws scientifically. The ancients could have used the radio, television, telephone, automobile and airplane thousands of years ago, but their minds were not ready to believe in the possibilities. The principle by which these inventions came forth always existed and could have been used.

Wear the Right Garment

A garment in the Bible is a mood, tone, vibration or attitude of mind which you wear. For example, taking it literally for a moment, if you are a private in the army and go to the king wearing the uniform of a private, you may be sent to do latrine duty. If you go before the king wearing the garment of a general, you will get an appropriate assignment. If you go as a slave you will get more work to perform as a slave. If you are about to visit a very prominent person such as a queen or the President of the United States, you wear wonderful and expensive clothes. You may not be particular whether your clothes are pressed or perfect, however, in the presence of a maid or other servant.

Spiritually speaking, every night as you go to sleep you visit the King of Kings, the Lord of Lords—the God-Presence. What kind of garment do you wear as you go into the deep of sleep? The Psalmist says: *Enter into his gates with thanksgiving, and into his courts with praise: be thankful unto him, and bless his name. For the Lord is good; his mercy is everlasting; and his truth endureth to all generations* (Psalm 100:4–5).

A woman living here in Leisure World was much perturbed about a protracted lawsuit. Her prayer during the day and prior to sleep was: "Thank you, Father, for the Divine solution." She repeated this over and over again, and she lulled herself to sleep every night with the feeling of thankfulness for the happy ending. The woman who had instituted legal proceedings against her passed on quietly in her sleep, leaving a note addressed to her asking for forgiveness and directing a cancellation of the law suit. Apparently this woman knew she was about to pass on to the next dimension.

You can never know how your prayer will be answered. The thankful heart is always close to God. Never go to sleep with the feeling of resentment, anger or condemnation, because your subconscious magnifies what you deposit in it. Your subconscious acts on the engraving made by your conscious mind.

Your Subconscious Mind Is No Joker

A woman told me an interesting story about her deceased sister. Apparently their father had said to their mother in the presence of the two girls, "You are so old, I am leaving you for another woman," which he did in short order. She distinctly remembered her sister saying, "If that is what happens to you when you are forty, I will die when I am forty years old," and she did die on her fortieth birthday. She could have changed it by affirming long life, peace and happiness or by engraving the great truths of the 91st Psalm in her subconscious.

Watch Your Words—They Are Creative

Frequently I have heard the expression, "I'm happy in spite of, not because of." You must be happy because of. . . . *Whoso trusteth in the Lord, happy is he* (Proverbs 16:20). . . . *He that keepeth the law, happy is he* (Proverbs 29:18).

If, for example, Jones across the way is out of a job and you say, "Well, I'm better off than he is. At least I am working. I'm happy and I will be happy in spite of the conditions around me," you are acknowledging lack. You are being stoical about it. You must be happy because you have decreed happiness, peace and abundance. All these come from contact with the God-Presence within you.

When your mood is natural, you do not at the same time become conscious of lack all around you and dwell on that because that is a mood, too, and you express it. How do you pray? Do you go within and say, "Well, I will get into the mood, but I don't think it's possible." That's a mood, too. That is the garment you wear. Do you go within and say, "Well, it might happen in the near future. I'll condition it in the future." That is a mood or feeling. Or do you go within and say that it is a fact and galvanize yourself into the feeling of being it or possessing it. This is called in the Bible *Jericho*—the fragrant state, or the joy of the answered prayer.

The Power Within You

In the army I knew a man who, by means of a forked hazel stick, could tell by its pull toward a spot in the ground where water could be found, no matter how arid and unlikely a place it seemed to the senses. He was born in Australia, and his father had possessed that gift, as did his grandfather. Both had told him that he had the gift also, a statement which he accepted and believed. According to his belief was it done unto him. He did not find it strange to feel the pull of the hazel stick, which was but a means of tapping his subconscious mind, which knows all and sees all. There are a great many dowsers, as they are called, who can find oil, water, etc., by means of a forked hazel stick, or even a wire coat hanger.

When you have faith and confidence that you will find water or oil, your subconscious will respond accordingly. Moreover, if you implicitly believe, like this young Australian, that the gift is transmitted from father to son, your subconscious will respond accordingly.

Promote Yourself

I told a young banker who had been very successful in his work but who had not been promoted in ten years that he should promote himself. I suggested using the following technique: Every night prior to sleep to practice the following proposed action, which would ordinarily follow the fulfillment of his desire. He was to feel himself participating in the action with the vividness and distinctness of reality. He imagined the president of the bank shaking hands with him and congratulating him on his outstanding promotion. He placed his hands in the hands of the president, feeling them to be solid and real, and carried on an imaginary conversation in harmony with the congratulatory message.

He did this in his own room, making there here and the future now. Mentally and spiritually, the president was present in his room, and he heard his voice distinctly congratulating him on his good fortune. You do not visualize yourself at a distance in point of space, such as being in the other person's home; neither do you dwell upon distance in point of time. Make elsewhere here and the future now. Remember that the future event is a reality now in a dimensionally larger world. There is no time or space in the Mind-Principle.

Realize the difference between feeling yourself in action here and now and visualizing yourself as though you were on a motion picture screen; that is the difference between success and failure. Imagine someone right in front of you, someone who would love to hear good news about it, and have this person tell you over and over again what you long to hear.

That is a wonderful way of impregnating your subconscious mind.

This young banker, who continued practicing the technique outlined for two weeks, had it confirmed objectively when he was called in to the head office and promoted to position of bank manager of one of the big banks. He confirmed objectively what he had imagined and felt subjectively.

The following is a good prayer for your business: "I now dwell on the omnipresence and omniaction of God. I know that this Infinite Wisdom guides the planets on their courses. I know that this same Divine Intelligence governs and directs all my affairs. I claim and believe that Divine understanding is mine at all times. I know that all my activities are controlled by this indwelling Presence. All my motives are Godlike and true. God's wisdom, truth and beauty are being expressed by me at all times. The All-Knowing One within me knows what to do, and how to do it. My business or profession is completely controlled, governed and directed by the love of God. Divine guidance is mine. I know God's answer, for my mind is at peace. I rest in the Everlasting Arms."